QUESTIONABLE COMMENTARY

LATE-ONSET CONTEMPLATIONS FROM
AN EAST COAST SEPTUAGENARIAN

William J. Kilfoil

◆ FriesenPress

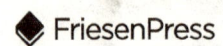

Suite 300 - 990 Fort St
Victoria, BC, V8V 3K2
Canada

www.friesenpress.com

Copyright © 2020 by William J. Kilfoil
First Edition — 2020

All rights reserved.

No part of this book may be reproduced or transmitted in any form or by any means without written permission from the author.

No part of this publication may be reproduced in any form, or by any means, electronic or mechanical, including photocopying, recording, or any information browsing, storage, or retrieval system, without permission in writing from FriesenPress.

The articles reproduced here (with minor edits) were originally published in the Halifax Chronicle Herald and/or in other Saltwire Network newspapers in Newfoundland, Labrador, and Prince Edward Island (2018-2020).

The scene depicted on the front cover is an acrylic painting (by the author) of Mitchell's Cove in Oyster Pond Jeddore on Nova Scotia's beautiful (but unsung) Eastern Shore.

ISBN
978-1-5255-7350-7 (Hardcover)
978-1-5255-7351-4 (Paperback)
978-1-5255-7352-1 (eBook)

1. LITERARY COLLECTIONS, ESSAYS

Distributed to the trade by The Ingram Book Company

For   Celeste Yvonne

        Kara Anne
        Matthew Vincent
        Mark William
        Colleen Jeanette
        Kimberley Marie
        Brennan Patrick

        All of our grandchildren

The photograph above, The Author at Work, *was taken on August 28, 1955, on the same day that a black American—fourteen-year-old Emmet Till—was tortured and murdered in Mississippi for making a saucy comment to a white woman.*

PREFACE

Thoughtful folks recommend against unauthorized commentary and amateur memoirs, especially those recalling experiences that were ordinary and tedious at the time but, in hindsight, were fancied as thrilling and engaging by an aging writer.

Some suggest that seniors who feel compelled to record opinions and perceptions gleaned from an earlier life be reminded that two advantages are gained from putting off such writings for as long as possible: The first benefit is that the project may be forgotten about and abandoned altogether. The second advantage is that the risks involved in pruning and polishing one's recollections will inevitably be reduced as potential challenges to personal accounts obligingly die off––with condolences and respects duly paid––in time for publication.

This book ignores that advice, documenting assorted opinions and perceptions from an old guy on Canada's East Coast. The commentary is occasionally instructive, but more often light-hearted and unserious. The author's hope and intention is to evoke a smile and convey affection for community and family, and the decencies that allow them to flourish.

The perspective is that of a late-onset chronicler with questionable insight, scant writing experience, and no claim to represent peers except through the acknowledged community of retirees who get up twice a night to pee.

The commentary is served up with humour, nostalgia, and some bologna. A grain of salt is recommended. Readers who can't get through the entire book should throw it in the garden shed where the squirrels can chew on it. See if they can finish it.

-William J. Kilfoil

TABLE OF CONTENTS

PREFACE	vii
ABOUT THE NEIGHBOURHOOD	**1**
A Dog's Breakfast	2
Growing Tired	5
Measuring Mania	7
Google Home Invasion	10
The Real McNeil	13
HOLIDAYS	**17**
Knitting Christmas	18
Gifts from My Barber	20
Perilous Presents	22
Geriatric Resolutions	28
Remembrance Day Turbulence	31
December 2018	34
Eclipsing the Moon	37
The Two-Faced Season	39
OLD-SCHOOL STUFF	**43**
Molasses	44
Loretta Leaks	46
Pencils Reconsidered	49
Mrs. Gannet's Grammar	52
Learning by Heart	55
Chocolate Maps and Pointy Sticks	60
Assassination and Confession	62
Nuns, Law and Order	66
Soothing September	68
Sticking Up for the Irish	71
Trump and My Mother	73

FOGGY RECOLLECTIONS — 75
Writing Stuff Down — 76
The Sixth Toe — 80
Smoking in the Glory Days — 83
Quantifying Happiness — 88
Newspapers: An Elegy — 91
Scanning the Obits — 94

GETTING OUT OF THE HOUSE — 97
Carnivores and Other Sinners — 98
Wing Night — 99
Eating Out — 103

CHEWING THE RAG — 107
Sense and Humour — 108
Tim's Tidbits — 110
Contrarian's Summit — 112
Observations from the Corner Booth — 115
Goat Yoga — 117

ASSORTED RUMINATIONS — 121
Turning 70: The Side Effects — 122
Satisfaction Levels — 124
Elusive Truth — 127
Awaiting My Epiphany — 130
Humility: Still a Virtue — 133

ABOUT THE NEIGHBOURHOOD

A Dog's Breakfast

My wife and I live in a residential community of walkers and step counters, a pleasing, contented neighbourhood featuring several species of pooches and pensioners.

Most days, agreeable folks walk around our quiet streets accompanied by their dogs, or if the dogs aren't available, by their spouses. Folks strolling around the neighbourhood whose names are not known to us are identified by their canine companions — *you know the one I'm talking about: the blonde lady with the golden Lab.*

Like many suburbs, we benefit from dog diversity. We have dogs of every breed, creed, and political persuasion (including a brown-faced variety called Trudeau terriers). We have dogs that are faithful, promiscuous, atheists, disciples, lifters and squatters, pacers and trotters. We have four-legged, two-spirited dogs. Some are lumpy, some smooth, some are as fat as a home-plate umpire, and some as thin as a coat hanger. We have capitalist and socialist dogs, uplifting dogs, downward-facing dogs, newly minted dogs and ancient dogs—some can hardly lift a leg to pee. Some are more sophisticated than others—one cocker spaniel has a Facebook page, and a few Nova Scotia retrievers have a Twitter account for trolling ducks.

Almost all of them are civilized, well-mannered, middle-class dogs––no aristocrats. None live in a purse or are carried under the arm of a bejewelled woman dressed in fur. These are courteous, agreeable dogs. When their owners meet other walkers on our road and say, *"It's a lovely day,"* their dogs nod in agreement. They have names like Henry, Charlie, and Skipper. Most are trained only to growl at Liberals and vegetarians. One ill-tempered dog named Cromwell barks exclusively at Irish people and atheists.

Some eat organically and chew only on bones grown locally. None of our neighbourhood dogs wear a Fitbit or use a step counter (would it multiply by four?), and when they get tired of walking, they sit down—evidence that they are smarter than the ones at the other end of their leashes. These dogs are generally healthy, and are useful in a variety of ways (dogs can find anything — Meghan and Harry are bringing along their beagle and black Lab to help them find financial independence in Canada, and the beagle can help with security). A few yappy dogs are suffering from attention deficit disorder, some are neurotic, and some are on medication. A few of these dogs are hypochondriacs (let loose, they run to the vet for every little thing).

We have multicultural, free-thinking dogs unfettered by custom and convention. Mainlanders own Newfoundland dogs named Crosbie or Smallwood. Not all the Irish setters support the Republic, not all the bull terriers are monarchists. The sheepdogs do not flaunt their intellect. The black dogs are not all depressed. One neighbourhood dog recently emigrated from China, her arrival unsullied by tariffs or balance-of-trade issues. Since her arrival to Canada, Penny (from Hang Zhou, population nine million) has not spoken a word of Mandarin Chinese. She has made new friends, has joined the kennel club, and is now fully integrated into our quiet suburban neighbourhood.

For the most part, dog owners take care of business. Even those who are careful to sanitize the handle of their shopping carts at Sobeys have no trouble stooping to the shoulder of the road to collect their dog shitzu in inverted blue bags. You have to appreciate this.

My wife and I do not own a dog in a community where everyone else does. We are outliers and therefore unqualified to comment on the virtues and consolations of dog ownership.

My limited knowledge of canine attitudes and behaviours was heavily influenced (years ago) by a high school teacher who believed that the reason dogs were put on this Earth was to enrich the English language. He also believed that—through dog-related idioms, metaphors, and figures of speech—bountiful canine wisdom is imparted to civilization.

This eccentric English teacher was named Thomas Bernard. He was a bachelor who shared living space with a golden Labrador named Nipper. When he wasn't talking about Nipper, Mr. Bernard taught us English literature. He told us with pride how he read *The Chronicle Herald* to his dog in the evenings after supper––and before bed, some Shakespeare.

The most memorable thing about Mr. Bernard was that he thought the wisdom of the ages could be summed up in a few dog clichés. Although most of his stuff was hackneyed and well-worn, he was relentless; he couldn't lay off the dog references. He was like a dog with a bone.

Some days, he had a hang-dog face (when he was dog-tired), but most of the time, he was as happy as a butcher's dog. He didn't want you missing any time unless you were as sick as a dog, but when you came back, he claimed he hadn't seen us in a dog's age. He advised against putting on the dog.

Politicians were as crooked as a dog's hind leg. His aunt Mary was so ugly he wouldn't take her to a dog show (for fear she'd win). When his feet were sore, his dogs were barking. He referenced a dog-eared dictionary (the library was down the hall, dog-leg to the left) and he loved the dog days of summer. If we passed in an incoherent paper, it was labelled "a dog's breakfast;" if we complained about a mark, we were "barking at the moon." A weak excuse drew a comment like "that dog don't hunt" or "we should be careful what we ask for because any dog that will give you a bone will take one away. And don't be like a dog chasing a mail truck; you might catch up to it, but then what?"

Mr. Bernard also had dog parables, raising dog wisdom to biblical proportions. Although he gave us a lot of freedom (a dog let to run loose isn't as likely to run away), he advised us about the dangers of stipulated reality. "You can't just make stuff up," he'd say. Mr. Bernard had a riddle to illustrate this truth.

"Tell me this," he'd say. "If you call a tail a leg, how many legs does a dog have?" He then assured us that the answer is four (not five), because "calling a tail a leg doesn't make it one." Apparently, you can't make something true just by saying it is. This is irrefutable dog wisdom. (At the time, it didn't seem profound, but these days, a few political types would do well to remember it.)

Mr. Bernard also cautioned us about the nature of gratuitous criticism. We should be careful when casting aspersions, he said, because "If you kick a dog in the ass, you had better be prepared to deal with her teeth. It's a dog-eat-dog world."

Mr. Bernard was a saint. He always wore a hound's-tooth jacket. It's unfortunate he wasn't allowed to wear a small keg of brandy around his neck.

At home, my desk faces the street. During the time I write this prattle, three dog walkers have passed my window. The first is a young woman who lives on the next street over. I can't remember her name—Mary Something. Her white dog looks like a little lamb and follows her everywhere.

Not long after, a friend of mine is passing by with his Shetland sheepdog named Gibson. Gibson is taking his owner (a Cape Bretoner) for a walk, teaching him the route and who's in charge.

Gibson and his relatives (the Shelties) get along well with the McGregors, the McDonalds, the McIntyres, and other highland clans because of their shared geography. Gibson's canine ancestors are from the Shetland Islands in the most northerly part of Scotland. Gibson and his proprietor share a natural affinity for parsimony, sheep, and Scotch (just a wee drop taken, you know, hair of the dog). Gibson takes care of his owner. His genetic heritage has taught him to retrieve errant sheep back to the flock.

Recent research indicates that over time, dogs and owners begin to share personality traits. They not only start to look like each other, they begin to act like one another — mutually influenced by the aggression, equanimity, or indifference shown by the other. Apparently, a thoughtful dog can make you a better person.

Gibson and his master are well groomed, properly shorn, and reasonably healthy, but both are accumulating years faster than they'd like. So far, neither of them sheds or drools, but this will come soon enough. They watch what they eat. Both are non-smokers. There is some potential for weight gain. They share a conservative perspective. Gibson doesn't mind barking at dogs bigger than he is. He barks truth to power.

At the other end of our street, a friend of mine shares living space with a chocolate Lab. Roxy is a lovely dog—portly, lumpy, and flatulent. She doesn't bark much anymore—Roxy has learned about the indifference of the world; nobody's listening anyway. She is wise and insightful, and she has a sense of humour. She lives a dog's life without objection. She knows people are flawed, but doesn't worry about it.

Some days, Roxy looks tired, because (like me) she is afflicted by old age and inertia. At home, she lies on the floor shedding hair, farting, and lumbering from one room to another. Roxy is my favourite dog. Roxy and I are kindred spirits.

Growing Tired

I suppose it's considered heretical among orthodox horticulturists, but I'm just not that interested in gardening anymore, and prefer to spend my time reading or complaining. Also, I've noticed that garden-variety vegetables can be found around the perimeter of any Sobeys store, at what seems to be a reasonable price, especially if you factor in the capital and operational costs of backyard production (tillers, hoes, rakes, fertilizers, Veseys seeds, Robaxacet, etc.). Coming from generations of Irish potato growers, I feel a bit guilty about my non-participation. I also understand that seniors are supposed to be interested in gardening, not least because it is one of the few things that we get better at as we get older (there aren't many). The only other improvement is an enhanced capacity for not worrying about what other people think.

My wife, Yvonne, talks to me about our garden, hoping to get me interested and involved. Her words fall by the wayside on stony ground and yield no fruit. When I discussed my agricultural apostasy with my friend Albert, he was properly empathetic. Albert indicated that he, too, prefers to avoid the garden path in order to cultivate the mind, to grow the garden within. This perspective means that Albert and I are sluggish, have neither the patience nor flexibility the activity requires and, allegedly, more important things to do. Nonetheless, we both acknowledge that gardeners everywhere are rightly recognized for preserving the oldest and purest human pastime. They deserve a place in the sun.

Yvonne is a serious gardener, a campaigner for fresh vegetables and a grow-local crusader. By "local," I mean our backyard––there are no NIMBY protestors when it comes to gardening. For her, it's not just a pastime, but more of a genetic imperative strengthened by childhood experiences, growing up on a farm, and hours spent weeding, thinning carrots, hoeing potatoes, and spreading manure till the cows came home. Everyone contributed––the rows were long and tough to hoe––and everyone knew the drill. Happier hours were spent sitting at the kitchen table shelling peas and snapping beans. There was a small brush by the kitchen sink to get at the dirt under your fingernails.

For many, gardening is a compulsion with health benefits. Psychologists suggest horticultural activity is therapeutic, and the existence of a garden patch behind the house indicates good health, salubrious for both body and soul. And some say planting seeds is a compelling metaphor––it amounts to believing in tomorrow. Apparently, a gardener's heart is a poet's heart.

If only for the alliteration, my wife prefers Superstore Sheep Shit and Hoes from Home Hardware––and bags of topsoil as cheap as dirt. This year she's planted beets, peppers, tomatoes, and carrots. And like W.B. Yeats, she has nine bean rows there––but no wattles, nor hive for the honey-bee. At the end of each row of carrots, a stick is pushed into the ground. She takes a carrot-and-stick approach to encourage vegetable growth. Any unused space in the garden is planted with flowers. Decisions about planting flowers are not cut and dried. The Dithering Delphinium must be planted between a rock and a hard place, and the Bleeding Hearts belong in the Liberal section.

Later this summer, Yvonne will send our grandchildren to the garden, instructed to pull a single carrot, wash some of the dirt off in the rain barrel, rub it on the grass, and eat it. You can't do that at Sobeys. In the produce section, when children chew on the vegetables, the reaction is unfavourable.

I am told that the green movement and other legislative initiatives have spawned a new generation of gardening enthusiasts. Maybe so. Earlier in the summer when my wife and I dropped into a local nursery to pick up a dozen tomato transplants, there was a conscientious young man there, working alone. He was body-pierced and heavily tattooed, and seemed pleasant enough but a little confused when we asked for twelve tomato transplants. He said we couldn't get a dozen, we are only allowed to grow four plants per household––for recreational use only––and to be careful around children and pets. We explained that we wanted twelve tomato plants, and after some clarification and amusement, we paid for the tomatoes, as well as some peppers and onions, and headed home. My wife says that's not exactly how it happened. But (as Dylan says) I was with her when the deal went down.

Measuring Mania

As Dubliner Oscar Wilde supposed, sometimes old age is accompanied by wisdom, but more often it shows up by itself. And whether looking inward or outward, my mental notes indicate that Wilde was probably right. Old people don't have many answers; they just have stories––a lot of stories. Some of these stories are extraordinary; most of them are surprisingly dull.

This perspective is also held by Albert, my co-conspirator. Albert is not persuaded that practical and intellectual guidance can be gleaned from spending time with old guys busy reconciling the death of contemporaries, declining productivity, and indigestion. He is not worried that Geriatric wisdom will spawn a deluge of sagacity that threatens the prevailing silliness in the nation's legislatures and universities. Albert believes that he can justify his skeptical position because he is part of the demographic on which he casts aspersions. "The rule is," he says, "you're allowed to hit your own gang. And besides, age confers a broader liberty to say what you think."

On Tuesday I ran into Albert at Costco as we lined up patiently for the privilege of putting some pension money back into the economy. I needed some aspirin and new socks. These days, my socks are all exactly the same; I don't have time to waste matching pairs, and if one gets a hole in a heel, there's no need to throw them both out (I don't know why I didn't think of it years ago). I also picked up a bottle of ten thousand aspirin, the smallest quantity they had available. (I'm quite an important guy at Costco––an Executive Member––every year I get a dividend cheque that pays almost half of my membership fee. It's worth it. They send me stuff in the mail. I get the catalogue and everything.) Albert was in the queue right in front of me. He was buying a five gallon jug of Windex, more than he will need in his lifetime. He uses it to clean his glasses. After expiration––his––Albert will leave the unused portion to his estate.

Albert and I are both past our best-before dates, but Albert's decline is strictly somatic; mentally, he's as sharp as ever. I always look forward to hearing his unvarnished point of view on current events, so we agree to meet in the parking lot and drive together over to Tim's for a bit of chewing the fat and coffee.

At first we are just relaxing, engaging in random talk with the unhurried aimlessness valued by children and Buddhists. Then Albert sees the man sitting at the next table getting up to leave and he notices that the poor guy is wearing a Fitbit on his wrist. Now Albert has focus––a switch is flipped. He wants to talk about the world's obsession with measuring everything. Once Albert builds up a head of steam he can get on quite a rant––he delivers more of a sermon than a lecture.

"These days, everyone's counting steps, and those skinny people with Fitbits on their wrist are starting to annoy me," he says. "We're obsessed with numbers, numbers and data–– 'metrics' we like to call them. We want to quantify everything: culture, intelligence, risk––even stuff that can't be measured. Economists have a metric to tell us how happy we are, Google counts our every keystroke, and Facebook records our every thought. Consumer monitors are disguised as air-miles cards, there's a camera on every corner, and face-recognition software knows when we skulk into the mall to use the toilet. Orwell had no idea. We have conceded any expectation of privacy. Did you see in the paper where insurance companies want access to Fitbit data? They're interested in knowing our blood pressure, our pulse rate, and when––for whatever reason––we might be doing a little heavy breathing. They may use the data to adjust premiums. We count people, cats, cars, money, body-fat index, and how many days left until Christmas. My dear old mother used to say, "Just count your blessings, that's where the counting begins and ends.

"But thanks to the data-generating capabilities of technology, we now substitute numbers for wisdom and insight. Of course, among advanced thinkers, wisdom is viewed with suspicion––especially when it is inherited or conventional wisdom. Among these towering intellects there is no greater shame than to be a thing of the past.

"A lot has been written about the difference between data and insight, but we don't seem to believe it. The fascination with data collection is unabated. We collect data about data––meta-data, micro-data, macro-data, and useless data. It's the tyranny of numbers. When we have enough data, we like to analyze it. We love to mine data. Mining data is big businesses. Occasionally it provides useful information. Apparently, impoverished governments can suffer from data deprivation, a condition requiring data innovation.

"Sometimes data collected by business and government leaches out into unwanted places; just ask Equifax, the FOIPOP people, or NS Health Authority. Conversely, data can also be hard to get at. One could imagine that data held by representative governments should be available to those they represent. Reading the paper this week, you might conclude that this is not the case. Nova Scotia's privacy commissioner was denied access to information held by the province's Health Minister. Perhaps anyone who wants to mine that data should contact natural resources. . ."

Albert paused for breath and coffee. I wanted to poke the bear, to keep him going. "So you're not a fan of the Fitbit thing," I said. He took a deep breath and started up again.

"The other day I was at Best Buy to pick up a printer cartridge––a new printer would have been cheaper––and a Nerd Squad guy came over and told me about those step counters. It does everything, he promised, alerts you to messages, takes your pulse, conferences with your computer, and even tells the time. Apparently the damn thing will let you know if you had a good night's sleep, and whether your heart stopped during the night. I told him that these functions were very impressive, and possibly useful. Especially the heart stoppage information––that would be something you'd like to know about right away."

The step-counting thing had Albert going; he was in full flight.

"There should be a law compelling walkers to look around and enjoy themselves, and throw the Fitbit in the harbour on the way by. And this obligation to "walk briskly" is starting to get on my nerves––can't we just go for a stroll? My advice is stop checking your watch, look around you, put one foot in front of the other, take that thing out of your ear and listen to the birds singing or the bus coming up behind you. Say hello to your neighbours when you meet *them* walking briskly, pet their dog. This will force them to stop and allow them to check their watch.

"And when, and by whose authority, was 10,000 steps decided upon as the targeted daily number? Are we sure it's not 8,537? And should the goal be seasonally adjusted, or indexed to inflation? Sure, it's good to get some exercise, but do we have to tally every goddamn stride? I'm pretty sure I walk 1000 steps every night getting up to go to the bathroom, but I won't be buying a Fitbit anytime soon. You can count on that."

Done his rant, Albert paused and drank his coffee. He was relaxed again.

We moved on to less compelling topics. Albert asked about a recent trip my wife and I had taken to the UK. "We spent an enjoyable evening in Cardiff," I told him, "where we met a local guide who was interested in numbers and sheep. The old gentleman explained to us that his country (Wales) has only three million people but ten million sheep. He went on to explain that the Welsh Department of Agriculture hired a census taker specifically to count the sheep, but the poor guy had a lot of trouble completing the job. He kept falling asleep."

I thought this was pretty funny. Albert laughed, but only slightly––a measured response.

Google Home Invasion

Recently my son––a technological wizard adept at all aspects of cyber-gadgetry––along with his wife and their three children, stopped by for a Sunday afternoon visit.

QUESTIONABLE COMMENTARY

Their baby is about eighteen months old, and just beginning to learn a few words. Apparently, babies tend to first learn simple words they hear most often in their home environment, especially if they are enunciated clearly and slowly.

So far our granddaughter can say "Mama," "Dada," and "A-Goog" (Hey, Google). This is not a word of a lie. These are her first words: *Mom, Dad,* and *Hey, Google*. God help us.

That same evening, I was next door visiting my neighbour, an older Nova Scotian like me. Our dialogue lubricated by John Jameson, we were sitting in the living room, chewing the fat. In the course of our conversation, we were talking about recent news items, including the Brexit debacle and the particular problems it poses for Northern Ireland. We were wondering about the number of people who lived in this part of the U.K. Neither of us was sure, so to demonstrate my worldliness and technological sophistication, I suggested we could just ask Google, and I went digging in my pocket for my iPhone.

But I wasn't quick enough. As soon as I uttered the words "ask Google," a very loud but otherwise pleasant female voice emanated from under the coffee table. There were only two of us in the room (or so I thought) and I wasn't expecting to hear from a third party. I was so startled I thought I might soil my boxers, but the danger soon passed and an omniscient female voice revealed that "the website World Population Review indicates that Northern Ireland has 1.8 million people, approximately 30 per cent of Ireland's total population and approximately three percent of the population of the United Kingdom."

Did I need any help with anything else?

Orwell had no idea.

After checking for any gastro-intestinal malfunctions and gathering my composure, I remembered that my neighbour had recently purchased a Google Home gizmo. But I was completely unaware that the thing was alive, awake, conscious, paying attention, and hanging on to my every word. I (perhaps naïvely) found this realization unsettling. I squirmed when I comprehended that the damn thing was listening and scrutinizing everything I said and every sound I made since coming through the front door an hour before.

What were the limitations of Google's omnipotence? How penetrating was her powerful ear? Did Google hear me clear my throat while I was ringing the doorbell––out there on the front step, did I mutter anything under my breath, and did I make any noises associated with digestion, gurgling, or worse?

After having learned about Northern Ireland from an unexpected source and pondering these questions, my neighbour and I regrouped and resumed our conversation.

But even with the help of JJ, I found it hard to relax. Google had interrupted us so suddenly, so unexpectedly, and so intrusively that I was still nervous about what had happened. I got the feeling the thing on the coffee table might not only be listening, but watching me, too, evaluating and recording my every move. For the remainder of my visit, I tried to avoid picking my nose or scratching myself, and I was careful not to ask about personal matters. The rest of the usually pleasant visit had an ominous "Big Brother" feel to it. Orwell had no idea.

A couple of days after the Google Home Invasion incident, I was online attempting to buy a pair of prescription eyeglasses (on the advice of a colleague who swears it is much cheaper). I never did go through with the purchase, but ever since I tried, I am bombarded with advertisements from Clearly (the eyeglass company) on every website I visit. The ads, like Mary's lamb, follow me everywhere I go.

Telling a (younger) friend about this, I was reminded that I'm a bit of a tech dinosaur, out of touch with the world of personal-data mining and directed intrusions. Apparently, the technologically astute know all about this business of targeted advertising, the abuses and misuses of Bookface, the relentless surveillance of the internet, and all the rest. These are not discretionary digital coincidences. It's all part of the apparatus of covert cyber reconnaissance.

I started reading a bit about these intrusions (online, of course, right beside the Clearly ads). Apparently, if you're over sixty-five and you ask Google what time it is, later that afternoon you'll get an email from Walmart telling you about special pricing on four-foot wall clocks. Or if you're talking to your wife on your iPhone and you tell her about a house for sale in the neighbourhood, in a couple of days you'll get a call from a real estate agent asking whether you are thinking about selling. And if you sneeze or cough out loud while you are reading this online material, you can anticipate a pop-up advertisement for Buckley's Mixture (it tastes awful, but it works).

Insurance companies want access to our Fitbit data so they can adjust premiums; shopping-mall cameras can now recognize our faces; Amazon (Am-is-on) is an expert on our personal interests and consumer habits; Bookface, a behemoth that knows more about us than we know about ourselves, has the evidence of our behaviours for sale; LinkedIn has several jobs waiting for us; if we watch a YouTube video called Health-Care in America, we might get a redacted email from Individual-One warning us about the dangers of socialism.

So my advice is to deactivate your smart doorbell, throw your Fitbit in the harbour, discard your Bluetooth ear buds, and if you want to talk to your wife about anything personal, go to the far corner of the garage and whisper quietly––or work out some system of sign language.

Expectations of solitude: conceded.

Both explicitly and implicitly, we allow intrusions unimaginable to George Orwell, and despite our protests, it's pretty clear we've conceded any prospect of confidentiality and, to some extent, waived our right to complain.

But I don't think we should give up on it. The whole abandoning-privacy trend is disconcerting. As when someone with otherwise sound judgment puts Pepsi in Irish whiskey, it's an indignity that's hard to overlook.

The reality is that sometimes Google (and others) is there with us, whether we know it or not, and whether we like it or not. Sometimes you just take another sip, assume a vacant look, and retire to the privacy of your mind, any expectation of solitude conceded, any hope of discretion abandoned.

The next time I went next door for a visit, I was suspiciously aware of that little white tower on the coffee table. I kept looking at it out of the corner of my eye. It appeared dormant, but I wasn't going to be fooled again.

I thought I might get used to it so that I could ask some questions. But so far, I just can't bring myself to look at that thing and say, "Hey, Google"––an utterance that is no trouble at all for a beautiful eighteen-month-old girl. But then again, probably not all eighteen-month-old girls can say "A-Goog." All of our grandchildren are well above average.

The Real McNeil

In our neighbourhood there are a significant number of retired folks who have so far resisted the inducements of communal living and the siren call of Baker Drive. For a while at least, we maintain home ownership, cut the lawn, and pay property taxes. Apparently there are some analysts who don't know the proper name for our segment of the population. We belong to the EONS (Elderly Ordinary Nova Scotians) who comprise a burgeoning demographic much talked about collectively, but whose members receive less attention individually.

Every year as spring threatens, the male of our species wanders around the neighbourhood looking for garage doors that are open. An open garage signals other male EONS to get out of the house. We want to chew the rag with other old guys who are tired of doing the cryptoquote. In our neighbourhood we tend to gather at Albert's garage. His door faces south. We sit just inside the door, in the sun but out of the wind, on wobbly lawn chairs. There is an old beer fridge at the back of the garage beside the table saw that hasn't been used since Albert retired.

EONS congregate in garages to engage in the discourse and disputation necessary to solve social and political problems on both a micro and macro scale. Our group, retired for years, consists of a couple of military guys, a high school teacher, a civil servant, a diesel mechanic, and a superannuated accountant. We are all curmudgeons, some more than others. On sunny afternoons we chew the fat and sip on a beer, maybe two. We are generally in good spirits. The conversation is unrestricted and coasters unnecessary. These seminars are never convened in the evening because we go to bed early. If there is a game on TV, we try to stay awake for the first period. In the morning we get up early to read the obituaries.

Last Saturday afternoon, Jim (military guy) dropped by the garage with a Sobeys bag that contained six Liberal Red IPAs––*The Real McNeil*––recently fermented and bottled in Cape Breton. The label featured a Bruce McKinnon caricature of our Nova Scotia Premier. Jim passed a beer to each of us. Then it started.

Apparently Big Spruce Brewing hoped their new IPA would promote constructive political engagement. They have no worries. When our commentary on The Real McNeil began in earnest, it was clear that improvements had to be made to the name. Alternatives were brought forward. Jim kicked it off with simple variations on the existing tag: Surreal McNeil, Repeal McNeil, Raw Deal McNeil, etc. More extensive name changes were suggested: Barley Balanced Budget Beer, The Unions Bitter, Clear-Cut Lager, and many others. Discussion continued at high levels. Improvements in nomenclature persisted, including suggestions based on McKinnon's long-faced caricature––Chins of the Father, Conjoined Chins, Bra Jaw Porter, etc.

QUESTIONABLE COMMENTARY

Jim, the most cantankerous of our group, offered surprisingly high praise. He said he was convinced that of all the craft beers ever brewed, The Real McNeil was not the worst. He was particularly amenable to its high alcohol content. He planned to take a case to his brother in Moncton, until he was reminded of the egregious crimes and punishments associated with inter-provincial beer trafficking. Bob led a discussion about appropriate packaging. Obviously, The Real McNeil was a tall boy and should come in a sixteen ounce can, and Dave suggested a better crock. Albert, a retired teacher, grunted that it left a bitter aftertaste.

Dave, a congenital Tory, recommended we imagine a brand named in memory of Jamie Bailey, whom he regretted was now absent from provincial politics. First Dave suggested a stout called Sans Jamie, which immediately mutated into JamieSans. This proposal was rejected by the group on the basis that JamieSans defamed the Dublin Whiskey we held in high regard. Dave settled on a brew called Jamie's Brow, a shiny expansive ale with a lingering presence. Albert thought N-Dipper Rev. Burris also deserved his own eponymous ale. He suggested a non-alcoholic beer called Social Ferment––indulgent yet reverential.

The beer commentary grew tiresome and was soon exhausted. We resorted to familiar conversations about visiting former workplaces, and how we didn't know anybody anymore, and how all the young people there imagine they have new ideas. And how Dave ran into so-and-so at the doctor's office the other day and my God he is starting to look old. EONS can converse intelligently on virtually any topic, but often revert to a standing agenda item related to establishing our own political party (EONS for an Idealized Past) with the slogan *Nostalgia ain't what it used to be*. Current politicians should take the threat seriously; EONS are ignored at their peril. We have time to plan the takeover. We don't have to go to work in the morning.

Just before we had to adjourn for supper, Jim's eighteen-year-old grandson dropped by the garage on his way home from SMU. Jim offered him a taste of The Real McNeil but his grandson declined saying he was afraid he might inadvertently read the label and be charged with some breach of privacy. The rest of us commented what a wise and prudent young man he was, although we expressed hope he would soon get a job and start paying taxes. These pensions aren't going to fund themselves.

HOLIDAYS

Knitting Christmas

Pastured somewhere in Cape Breton or the Scottish Highlands, dedicated and generous sheep are busy manufacturing wool.

Usually in the spring, these charitable animals willingly donate their outerwear sheerly to satisfy the demands of the numerous knitters, weavers, hookers, and textile fabricators whose numbers I understand are on the rise.

They are, like Christmas shoppers, seasonally fleeced.

My wife is a prodigious and compulsive knitter, especially in the pre-Christmas period when production increases dramatically — needles are airborne and scraps of yarn litter the floor around her rocking chair.

In our living room, the primary manufacturing sector is flourishing without government incentives or payroll rebates. We are currently at peak production.

For the most part, our grandchildren will be the beneficiaries come the New Year, warming their hands and heads with mitts and toques added to the basket by the back door, up until they are lost on the playground. They are children in sheep's clothing.

And this year, I'm getting a new pair of Newfoundland double-knit mittens (I know this because I had to try them on in mid-production), featuring extra warm design and a traditional trigger-finger pattern found in an entertaining and useful book my wife recently purchased, *Saltwater Mittens* (LeGrow and Scott*)*.

My mitts will have the old-style double construction, striped wrist, diamond back, and salt and pepper tops. The trigger-finger design is useful in the event I want to keep my hands warm while shooting a moose or playing the piano.

My wife can also knit dolls, scarves, sweaters, slippers, socks (reinforced heel and toe)––and her brow. And I'm pretty sure she could, if asked, knit me a table saw.

I know nothing about the process of knitting, and don't want to. I'm not at all clear about how a pair of perfectly formed mittens emerges from that peaceful activity in the rocking chair, but it's just one of the increasing number of deficits and obscurities I'm willing to live with. (I don't know how my iPhone works either, and I can't pronounce the word isthmus, even though I know we're connected to New Brunswick by one. And what the heck is a bitcoin anyway?)

So the chances of me looking at any publication about knitting are about the same as me forgetting to eat supper. But this latest book was an exception because it included several amusing anecdotes and quotes, including one from the gifted (now deceased) Newfoundland journalist Ray Guy, who helps me understand the concept of a shepherd: "We all knew what a shepherd was, any fool did. A shepherd was a person who had nothing to do except tend sheep, unless he was a woman, in which case he was a shepherdess. Shepherds were persons like Little Bo Peep and David who slew Goliath ..."

For my generation, wet wool is a powerful memory trigger— the smell of woolen mitts and hats on the hallway furnace grate at home, or thrown on the clanking, hissing cast-iron radiator in the cloakroom at school. The sizzle of the snow-encrusted mitts as they hit the hot surface, the steam rising with the aroma of wet wool drying ...

As a child, nobody I knew wore gloves or store-bought mitts. Every Christmas, my sisters and I received a brown-paper- wrapped parcel that came in the mail several days after Christmas was over. The package was from my Grammy and contained the same thing every year—mittens for everyone, a catalogue from Briggs and Little, and religious medals on chains that turned green when they got wet. Mine was a haloed Saint Joseph holding a woolly lamb, the Lord his shepherd.

There is some evidence that women can knit blind––or even while talking on the phone or watching TV. One Newfoundland story tells about a woman who knit two pairs of socks after she fell asleep in her chair. And another about an old woman who, after she died, had her hands tied in the coffin to keep them still until Sunday came around when, as everyone in Newfoundland knows, knitting is illegal.

Next year at Christmas, if I behave myself, I might get a pair of five-fingered mittens (gloves), or even better, a pair of Fogo Island Nine Patch.

Right now, my wife is in the living room multi-tasking: talking on the phone having a yarn with our Newfoundland neighbour, while watching the Weather Channel and knitting away. And I'm in the kitchen making tea when I drop a cup on the ceramic floor. It smashes loudly into a thousand pieces. I sense a cold front on the way.

I clean up the mess and announce that I'm going to bed. I have to get some sleep––to knit the raveled sleeve of care.

WILLIAM J. KILFOIL

Gifts from My Barber

Several remarkable events occurred in the fall of 1961. The East Germans began construction of the Berlin Wall, New York Yankee Roger Maris hit his sixty-first homerun in the last game of the season, and I got my first barber-shop haircut. I was twelve years old, in grade five, with Sister Donovan at the front of the room. It was a turning point. Up until December 1961, I had never been inside a barber shop. Until then, my father cut my hair at home to save us money. It was part of his plan to make sure we didn't end up in the poorhouse.

My father was a generous man, but his barbering techniques were cruel and unusual and later forbidden by the Geneva Conventions. My haircutting ordeal took place about once a month, usually on a Saturday night, when I was summoned to the kitchen, sat on a stool, and shrouded with an old bed-sheet last used when painting the hallway. A shoe box containing the hair-cutting implements was placed on the kitchen table. The kit had four components: a long thin comb, dull scissors, a can of three-in-one oil, and a pair of hand-squeezed manual hair clippers previously used to torture unbelievers during the Spanish Inquisition. My father could shingle a roof, but he had no training as a barber.

After a few drops of the three-in-one oil, he applied the manual squeeze-clippers (purchased from the Eaton's catalogue) to the back of my neck and high around my ears. Sometimes these clippers cut hair in the way they were intended, but mostly they just got a good grip on it, allowing my father to pull it out in clumps. He went at it in earnest, like he was weeding the garden. If I protested, the consequences were unfavourable, and when the operation was over, he proudly announced "you're done," as if he had just completed a liver transplant. He took the hair-littered bedsheet to the back step and shook it.

I slinked to the bathroom to look in the mirror, to survey the damage. It was clear that I had escaped from an oncology ward, having just finished the last of my radiation treatments. My mother said not to worry; it would grow back in no time, and in the meanwhile, it would be easier to keep clean. And she reminded me that vanity was a sin, which it was at the time. These consolations were not helpful. In the days following the haircut, I experienced mild symptoms of PTSD.

Hidden in the bathroom, I tried to moderate the mutilation by slicking back the remaining hair with Brylcreem, but ended up looking—as my mother said—like I had brushed my hair with a pork chop. Fortunately I had, in those days, cultivated forehead pimples, larger and more prominent than what you might imagine. These provided a valuable distraction to the white patches on my scalp.

But in December of 1961, God's mercy and compassion became more noticeable when my father decided he would stop cutting hair and let me go to the neighbourhood barbershop, where a boy's haircut cost a dollar. I think my mother talked him into it. I'm not really sure why my father gave in, but it was the Christmas season and maybe he was inspired to reveal a little more goodwill towards men (and boys). But more likely it was my mother's intervention. "He's old enough now; let him go to the shop," she said, "for Christmas." I did go, and my father never cut my hair again. It was the greatest Christmas gift bestowed since the Magi visited Bethlehem.

My hairstyling requirements were transferred to Harold's Barber Shop, open until noon on Saturday. Harold had a sign in the front that said *Haircuts While You Wait*.

Harry was an unimproved name for a barber, and every boy who went to see him told him that they wanted just a little trim, but Harry cut hair so that the fathers would think they got their money's worth. Harold knew where the dollar came from. The result was often a little shorter then I would have liked, but there was no physical pain involved and no bald patches. There were a number of reasons why I would never complain. Harry was old and a bit cranky, and I was reluctant to awaken any violent tendencies by voicing any displeasure with the result. My jugular was right there by his elbow, and the straight razor within easy reach. When it was over, Harry massaged my brain with some funny smelling treatment from a gallon jug, and then he splashed cheap cologne on my neck. My mother said it made me smell like an Anglican bishop. I'm not sure what she meant. The mystique of the cologne was the best part.

Prior to the barbering emancipation of '61, no turning points in my life were remembered. I don't think I experienced any childhood epiphanies and, as far as I know, no barriers were broken down, no taboos trampled on. The Christmas haircut of '61 stands out.

Thinking back on it now, I realize that I shouldn't have been so worried about my hair in the first place. Thanks to my Irish heritage (genes donated by both my parents), my hair wasn't much to begin with—thin, weak, and wispy, to go along with the other Irish compensations of pale freckled skin, big feet, and weak lungs. Everyone knows the Irish wear tweed as a remedy for dandruff.

And, over the years, the relationship between me and my hair has gone steadily down the drain to the point where it can no longer be rehabilitated. Suffice it to say, we've had a falling out. Apparently one of us had to go. And so far I've endured, although it isn't clear for how long.

Perilous Presents

My father would never throw away a pair of socks until there was a hole in both of them.

You'd think that paired socks would tend to wear out at about the same time, but this is not the case. Sometimes, it takes months for the other heel/toe to poke through. And my father's sock policy was indifferent to the fact that every year at Christmas he got more socks than you could shake a stick at.

Father was a Sabbath-keeping, non-coveting man with fewer rattles in his head than most. He didn't have much or want much (just a little peace and quiet), but, as concerns his wardrobe, he carried a disproportionate inventory of socks—beautiful store-bought socks from his children and heavy wooden socks from my mother—an embarrassment of socks that overflowed from a basket on his bureau.

One Christmas, my father didn't get socks. That year, my mother bought him a flannel shirt with a blue/green Scottish plaid. She explained that it was a Campbell Tartan. My father wouldn't wear it because of what happened at Glencoe in 1692.

Christmas memories adhere. And while older folks tend not to remember much about last December, they have no trouble reaching back to childhood experiences when some families went together to midnight mass and came home to find shards of ribbon candy and the detritus from shelled walnuts on the kitchen table beside a pair of pliers.

And in the morning, the shells and pliers were gone, replaced with short-bread crumbs and a half glass of milk, and an orange in the toe of a woollen sock. And later, at dinner, the wonders of the cranberry sauce, stuffing, and gravy. And how will we decide who gets to pick the pope's nose? And don't forget to put the wishbone above the stove to dry.

The baking frenzy goes on for days (my father said it was quite a carry-on)— the alchemy of mother turning sugar and flour into gold, creating shortbread and mincemeat pie with the redemptive power to convert Scrooge to a philanthropist and infuse hearts with noble sentiment.

Kids are thinking about gifts, though.

We're told giving stuff away is better, but (for children especially) gifts received also leave a mark. In our house, in early days, Santa manufactured a lot of the stuff we got for Christmas; but later, Santa had to order from the catalogue of the T.E. Eaton Company, which could supply every earthly comfort and every manufactured item available in Western civilization.

The pictures in the Eaton's catalogue were wonderful, and the range of products was staggering. You could buy everything from refrigerators to grease guns, to what my uncle called "women's under harness."

Somewhere in the haze of long-ago Christmases, Santa Claus (working in concert with Timothy Eaton) provided me with the extraordinary gifts described below. Each of these delivered the excitement and the trauma necessary to ensure they would never be forgotten.

Here's the story.

Annually, my father delivered his seasonally adjusted messages related to the purpose of Christmas, and the imperfect benefits provided by material things, and the reasons why unfettered consumerism and crass commercialism needed to be guarded against—especially at Christmas, when retail armies were set loose.

Notwithstanding his cautionary message, one particular year it was explicitly understood that my sister and I could each ask (Santa or his agents) for Christmas gifts with a total cost of less than twenty dollars.

There is a reason I remember this ceiling on expenditures.

To get her money's worth, my sister (after anguished equivocation) chose a Parcheesi game, a View-Master, and two Nancy Drew books.

Not me. I had discovered in the Eaton's catalogue a leading-edge technology with which I was fascinated, and I was willing to forgo all other Christmas presents—for several years, if necessary—if only I could have the small four-transistor reel-to-reel tape recorder pictured there, with two spools about two inches in diameter wound with a thin magnetic tape. The catalogue promised that this technical marvel would record about ten minutes of sound. The price was $19.95—just under the wire.

For me, the idea of recording music and voices held great appeal, valuable as entertainment as well as gathering evidence. I made it clear to everyone that if this extraordinary gift was bestowed, it would satisfy all my heart's desires, not just this Christmas but probably for the rest of my life.

In the days leading up to Christmas, I was overflowing with goodwill towards men (especially toy manufacturers), but I had no hint from anyone as to whether my fervent wish would be granted. I was nervous about it and decided to take matters into my own hands. Excitement impaired my judgment.

A couple of days before Christmas, Ma and Pa had gone out, visiting at my uncle's house. My sister and I were left home to babysit. The younger kids were in bed when I convinced my sister we should pass the time by snooping around the crannies and closets of the house, looking for locations where Christmas gifts awaited distribution.

She agreed reluctantly. The situation was tense. We knew that if evidence of our explorations was detected, it would jeopardize the receipt of the gifts we were hoping to find.

We moved stealthily, listening for the sound of the car in the driveway. I knew what I was looking for. It didn't take long.

A small cardboard box from Eaton's was exhumed from the attic under the eaves of the roof. I carefully removed the recorder from the box, held it in my wobbly hands, and relished my inauguration into the age of miracle and wonder.

I fiddled with the controls while my sister fidgeted and whispered nervously. When my inspection was complete, I carefully put everything back in order in the attic among the other gifts. The crime scene was examined. No culpable evidence was left, no fingerprints. My heart was full.

Two days later, on Christmas Eve, I was glad to be early to bed. I climbed the wooden hill and lay on top of the blankets, pretending to be asleep. I turned off all the lights and listened until I heard activity in the kitchen below, and crept down the hallway to the bathroom and kneeled at the heating grate, an opening in the floor that allowed heat from the kitchen stove to reach the upstairs. I could hear and even see (within a very limited range) what was going on.

My parents were wrapping gifts at the kitchen table. Dad was eating one of the cookies left for Santa and pouring milk back into the bottle so it wouldn't go to waste. My father, sharing my interest in the emerging world of technology, was examining the tiny tape recorder.

He casually pressed the "Play" button. A great darkness fell over the Earth. Out of the small speaker could be heard voices—children's voices faithfully reproduced, whispering "…did you hear that…we gotta get this thing back in the box before they get home…" The voices belonged to me and my sister.

I nearly shit my pants.

Terrified, I pulled back from the grate, tiptoed down the hall, crawled into my bed, pulled the covers to my chin, and lay still as a stick. I was clinically dead. The wind was rattling the loose-fitting storm windows, lace curtains trembled. There was furry frost at the bottom of the glass.

I had lost all my mirth. The magnitude of the situation paralyzed me. There was no way out. The evidence was irrefutable, more convincing than a DNA sample, my guilt beyond dispute. My gift, conceived to secure my happiness, instead provided the incriminating evidence I had imagined I would gather against others.

Heart-scalded, I was.

Holy Mary, pray for me at this hour of my death. I tried to make a deal with God: I would go to church every day for the rest of my life if God would just reverse time—go back three days—and we could start again. I knew God could reverse time if He wanted to. He could annul the laws of the universe on my behalf. It didn't seem too much to ask.

Then I heard my mother and father laughing. A great weight was lifted. Life returned and I went to sleep.

God didn't reverse time (as far as I know), but in the morning the wondrous tape recorder was under the tree. The evidence recorded therein was never mentioned, proof that God loved me and wanted me to be happy. His goodness and mercy had followed me.

For a brief period, I was grateful and I tried my best not to use my gift for evil purposes, although I often secretly taped my sister while she was talking on the phone.

The Christmas before the tape recorder debacle, Santa Claus had (without thinking it through) provided me with a woodcarving set. This offering consisted of a dozen razor-sharp blades that could be inserted into a handle that allowed ten-year-olds to carve a statue of David or perform open-heart surgery.

On Christmas morning—having no frogs to bisect or livers to transplant—I decided to whittle the edge off a pine board while supporting it on my knee. Predictably, and with surgical precision, I immediately executed a deep, clean incision through my Roy Rogers Christmas pyjamas, deep into my upper thigh. At first, the laceration hardly hurt, and I didn't want to interrupt my mother who was in the kitchen preparing the Christmas dinner, so I didn't mention it.

I changed my mind a minute later when the entire leg of my cowboy pyjamas turned dark red, and blood started dripping on the faded linoleum floor.

When she saw the slash on my thigh, Mother said, "Jesus Murphy"—more a prayer than a profanity—and she sprang into action, bringing all of her nursing training to bear on the crisis. Our medical supplies were kept in a shoebox in the kitchen cupboard. It was pressed into service.

In addition to gauze pads and adhesive tape, the shoebox contained iodine, goose grease, a blue bottle of Milk of Magnesia, Smith Brothers Cough Drops, a box of corn plasters, a St. Joseph's medal, and a thermometer. (I was aware that body temperature could be taken both orally and rectally, but only ever saw one thermometer.) Additional medical supplies included a red-hot water bottle that stayed hot for up to two minutes and leaked only a little.

The gash in my leg was clean and deep, about two inches long. It needed a dozen stitches, but Ma said that there was no need to drag a doctor out on Christmas Day—*he has a family, too, you know*—or impose a burden on a health system where, God knows, there was waste enough.

She had gauze pads and adhesive tape and nursing scissors from when she was in training. Ma knew how to make a poultice and she cleaned my leg wound and applied the absorbent gauze, secured with adhesive tape wrapped completely around my thigh.

I looked like a Passchendaele survivor. My mother was a saint. (Seeing that the breath of life remained in me, she bound up my wounds and restored me.)

The scar on my leg has shrunken a bit over the last sixty years, but I still have it—and, possibly, lingering PTSD.

The year after the tape recorder betrayal, Santa Claus (hoping to steer me into a career in engineering) provided me with a hazardous, but fully functional, miniature steam engine, my best gift ever.

It burned rubbing alcohol by absorbing it into cotton wicks, heating a boiler, producing enough steam to push a single piston and turn a miniature fly wheel. The piston puffed, the boiler hissed, the fly wheel squealed. It worked wonderfully. I loved it. I was part of the Industrial Revolution. I was James Watt.

The other thing I got for Christmas that year was an unexpected and confusing gift from my uncle: a briefcase with a locking mechanism (like the one on my sister's diary) and a key similar to the one my mother used to open canned meat (Klic or Kam). My uncle thought I needed the briefcase to carry my important papers. The lock would provide the necessary security.

On Christmas Day, the steam engine and the briefcase had an unanticipated encounter.

While running the engine in my room, performing a live refuelling manoeuvre, I spilled the bottle of rubbing alcohol. It caught fire and ran over the linoleum on the uneven floor. The flames spread across the room, exactly like they do in the cowboy movies when the bad guy pours kerosene to light the settler's cabin on fire.

The conflagration caused extreme but brief trauma, and it ended well—sort of. I managed (with startling and unforeseeable gallantry) to extinguish the fire with a bath mat even before my father reached the top of the stairs to see what the commotion was all about.

Nonetheless, his reaction was unfavourable. He did not seem to comprehend that my heroics had preserved the house that protected us from the chill winter winds and allowed for the survival of our family and all of our descendants.

Heart-scalded, I was.

With the fire extinguished, an inspection of the room revealed surprisingly little damage, with one notable exception. The burning alcohol had run up against my new briefcase, which was on the floor beside the table. I picked it up to look at it. This was the moment when I found out that my attaché was made of cardboard. It looked like a half-burned cereal box pulled from a depleted campfire. Thank God I hadn't yet put my important papers in it.

They age well, these glimpses from Christmases past. Fragments such as these are the gifts of the Magi. Wise men know it. And, as the old people understand, fragments of the past are the best we can hope for, and all we ever get, anyway.

Geriatric Resolutions

Recently, we were given a year's probation from the clutches and confinements of Christmas. Thus released, we are free to contemplate the New Year, or possibly the new decade—depending on your point of view. (The debate rages: Does a decade conclude with a year ending in 9 or a year ending in 0? We may have to go back to Anno Domini (AD) and exhume explanations from old monks with funny names like Dionysius Exiguus and Venerable Bede.)

We're not going to do that, because at this point in our current (Gregorian) calendar, custom and convention requires us to look not backward but forward, to focus on the future and consider improvements—to contemplate matters that need to be redeemed, renewed, reborn, or repainted.

That said, there are at least two of us who agree that no one over seventy should be allowed to make New Year's resolutions at all. People like us shouldn't even think about it. We know we're not going to change much, and if we do change, we didn't really mean to. Any self-administered attempt to modify our habits, demeanour, custom, and outlooks would be setting us up for failure. It would be like asking a sleeping cat to vacuum the living room (it wastes your time and annoys the cat) or inviting Senate Republicans to tell the truth. Recidivism runs high among us. Most of our days are essentially a repeat of the day before, with few renovations and few signs of evolution towards wisdom. Sure, we believe in paving roads and good intentions, but in the New Year, we support only modest and non-binding resolutions.

At least that was my and my friend Albert's position, when we were recently discussing these penetrating questions at our pensioners' breakfast at the IKEA cafeteria ($3.20, tax in). To get ready for 2020, we thought we should draft "Articles Guiding Resolutions for Seniors" (AGRS). Our first task was to establish unimpeachable terms of reference.

Article 1: The virtue of unambitious resolutions needs to be affirmed. Restraint is indicated. Large-scale improvements need to be guarded against. This regulation is justified by conventional wisdom (i.e. crawl before you walk, bark before you howl, old dogs and new tricks—all that stuff). The Queen of England agrees with us. On Christmas Day, during her annual yuletide message, Elizabeth II, in blue dress and pearls (a conspicuous member of the geriatric class), cautioned us that "small steps, not giant leaps" are what bring about lasting change.

QUESTIONABLE COMMENTARY

Therefore, in support of these principles (and the monarchy), resolution-declaring seniors endorse a prohibition on sombre and serious promises, and an embargo on resolutions such as those related to character improvements (it's too late), eating habits, lifestyle changes, weight loss, winter inertia, and the indignities of old age. Also, profound insights and high-minded discourse need to be avoided. If we can set aside these consequential matters, we have a chance to reflect on the bright and promising year ahead, full of hope and possibility.

Article 2: Thoughtful seniors should focus on modest, incremental corrections in two areas: sins of omission and sins of commission (bad stuff we do, and good stuff we don't do, but should). The catalogue might include performance related to areas such as the following: dryer lint removal, teabags in the sink, the seat up or down as required, rinsing before dishwasher loading, closing the cupboard doors, towel and shower maintenance, garbage day awareness, sandwich elements back in the fridge, dirty clothes put in the hamper, etc.

Article 3: Resolutions related to attitudinal changes are acceptable as long as everyone understands that improvements will be slight, if they occur at all.

Currently, Albert and I admit to unreasonably bad attitudes toward certain common behaviours: tipping at Tim Hortons; transporting turkey buzzards for medical treatment; retailers with no sense of humour; Christmas concerts, generally; people named after geographical features (River?); restaurant servers who ask if we have any plans for the weekend; drive-thru folks who tell us their name; stupid church signs; cable companies; power outage maps, and so on. We resolve to remediate these negative attitudes, fully aware we have no chance.

Article 4: Regarding media consumption in the New Year, Albert and I plan to pay more attention to Canadian news and far less to the gong show of American politics. In particular, we need to cut way back on the addictive, mind-numbing wasteland of CNN and establish a Trump-free zone as a refuge of sanity. Also, we need to be less cynical about the future of democracy, less pessimistic about the decline of post-factual America, and exhibit less contempt for the voters who populate that polarized wasteland. It's a tall order.

And locally, we must improve our attitude toward the pleasant and well-meaning people who deliver the (local) evening news. They are only doing their jobs, and I'm sure there is some market research to indicate they are doing it well. They are shiny, late-model hosts—well-mannered, attractive, and properly barbered.

But here's the thing: Some of these suppertime news-hour personnel are annoying us in more ways than we thought possible. ("They got me drove," as the Newfoundlanders say.) Some have accumulated an impressive repertoire of irritating behaviours, driving cranky people (like us) to hair-pulling distraction. On some evenings, both the substance and the delivery of the evening news contribute to aggravation in equal measure.

We're not sure what's worse: the paucity of news, the carrying on, the giggling, the nervous laughter, the affectations, the latest recycled YouTube video, the report on the relentless minutiae of talentless celebrity lives, the unremitting cuteness of cats and puppies, the irrelevant (yet viral) sensational behaviours caught on video, the affected empathy, the exaggerated interest, or the silliness. Not to mention the hosts imagining the viewer cares about their personal response to every single news item. And what about those surveys (purporting validity) that sometimes ask complex multidimensional questions (requiring nuanced answers) reduced to simplistic, multiple-choice responses (yes, no, maybe, don't know)? These are a suitable substitute for the other option which requires time and effort.

I can testify first-hand that, some days, the aggravation of the local news viewer finds full expression in a range of facial effects and descriptions unsuited for decent company (the man has a sailor's tongue in his head, so he has).

In the New Year, Albert and I need to stop disparaging these local productions. There's no need for it. We are probably outliers, whining, slow-witted curmudgeons put out to pasture. But still.

Article 5: Resolutions may also include a few things we are determined to learn this year—stubborn things we've tried to learn earlier but for some reason remain unclear to us (still hazy after all these years). This list is inexhaustible, but we touched on a few examples, such as: the electoral college, cryptocurrency, who made up that "10,000 step" baloney, what is the Privy Council, Bookface, the pronunciation of certain Gaelic phrases, the capital of the Netherlands, why eyeglasses are so expensive, is the evening meal supper or dinner, why did Tim's change the lid on the coffee, etc. (In the old days, a lot of this stuff I could ask my Uncle Eamon who knew everything—at least up until the visions started. He's dead now and unlikely to respond.)

When we got on the other side of our IKEA breakfast, we went back for a second cup (refills are free) and sat back down to review our work. We decided it had no value. It turns out our opinions are not necessary for the advancement of civilization. The "resolutions for seniors" project was overly ambitious. I withdrew my name from the documentation. It's now called "Albert's Resolutions for Seniors and Elderly" (ARSE).

Breakfast was good. The geriatric class can only do so much.

Remembrance Day Turbulence

On Friday, November 10, 1961, I was in grade six, attending a Catholic school, learning some manners and some geography, fully immersed in my formative nun-centered education.

This particular day was more memorable than it should have been, for two reasons. First of all, because the next day (Saturday) was Remembrance Day, we had a couple of unforgettable classroom visitors. And the same afternoon after our invitees left, I had to stay after school to apologize to Sister Donovan for the heinous crime described below.

On Friday morning, Sister Donovan told us about the guests we were expecting that afternoon: two elderly soldiers who had fought in the muddy trenches at Vimy Ridge during the First World War. She cautioned us that one of these gentlemen was in a wheelchair, having lost both his legs in the killing fields of France.

Sister Donovan, a former KGB agent who knew something about the proclivities and demeanor of twelve-year-old boys, issued a stern warning. We were counseled to be respectful, appear interested, ask questions, speak up, be polite, and avoid wiping our nose on our sleeves. These esteemed visitors had never been to our school before, and first impressions were enduring. The reputation of our school and the Roman Church hung in the balance. Regular lessons would be set aside.

When they arrived, the old soldiers had an impressive display of ribbons and medals dangling from their chests. One of them had trouble sitting up straight in the wheelchair.

Orders from Sister Donovan were followed until the introductions were complete, and then ignored. We twelve-year-olds didn't hear much of what the old soldiers said. They mumbled, we knew nothing of the places they mentioned, and we failed to show appropriate interest by asking questions. We just kept staring at the wheelchair, legs absent and pant legs turned up with safety pins.

We whispered to each other. None of us had any experience with hardship and sacrifice, let alone death and suffering. When the old soldiers left the classroom, Sister Donovan was pissed.

We thankless heathens had damaged the school's reputation by not showing proper respect for honourable men—complete strangers who had not been to our school before, they were leaving with a bad impression that could never be remediated.

None of us responded to Sister Donovan's admonitions. None, that is, except my friend Patrick. An eager boy, he meant no harm, but he could not sense danger—and he did not always think things through.

Patrick felt compelled to issue a rebuttal. "Yes, Sister," Patrick said. "They were strangers all right … but not *complete* strangers … because of … well … you know… the missing legs."

Sister Donovan said nothing. She just made the sign of the cross and went over and stared out the window. We thought she was having a stroke or an idea for a poem.

The previous week, Sister Donovan had begun teaching us a rudimentary understanding of the British Empire and its expansionist activities, including the establishment of African colonies. One passage in our textbook referred to Britain wishing to have a "place in the sun" — a metaphor, of course, meaning a prominent or favourable status among nations.

I asked Sister Donovan about the meaning of this phrase, "a place in the sun." She told me that Britain wished to develop additional colonies in sunny Africa and benefit from the favourable climate there—so unlike England, where it rained all the time. She didn't mention metaphor, or national pride, or international status; she focused on total rainfall amounts.

In those days, my father, who valued education and had a particular interest in history and geography, would occasionally monitor my homework. (Homework in every subject was not only allowed, but mandated.) After he listened to me recite the nine-times-table and my spelling list, my father started reading from my social studies textbook and asked me if I knew what was meant by the phrase "a place in the sun."

I told my father that earlier that day, I had put that very question to Sister Donovan and tried to give the impression that he had done well to come up with the same brilliant inquiry. I repeated what Sister Donovan had said, that the British, tired of the rain, were looking for a bit of sunshine in Africa.

"Don't be ridiculous," my father explained. He was annoyed, not that I misunderstood the metaphor but because he thought I was "careless with the truth" when I insisted that I was repeating exactly what Sister Donovan had said. His reaction was unfavourable.

In our house, untruthfulness was odious corruption, right up there with not making use of the gifts God gave you. My father reminded me that this virtuous nun was an intelligent, competent educator with over a thousand years of experience, and she certainly was familiar with metaphorical language and it would be an error to sully her reputation, impugn her authority, or question her genius.

My father was convinced that the infallibility of the pope in Rome flowed unimpeded through bishops and priests, to the nun in front of the blackboard.

He sent me to my room to reflect on the subtle distinction between what was said and what was heard, and to reconsider my position on the reliability of eyewitness testimony. And from Sister Donovan, I would ask for forgiveness. Unwilling to put my life and health at risk, I said nothing, went to my room and remained there for several hours under quarantine.

It was the following day, after the old soldiers left the classroom that I told my sad story to Sister Donovan and apologized, as my father directed. She did not acknowledge any error on her part.

I encountered a similar dilemma later that year in March, when Sister Donovan was talking about St. Patrick driving the snakes from Ireland. I had read somewhere that it was not St. Patrick but the ice age that drove the snakes away. I thought I should keep this information to myself.

And that evening at home, I knew that if I told my mother that St. Patrick was not Irish at all (born in Wales in Roman Britain), she might drop dead on the floor with no one left to cook my supper.

The world teaches you things, as my friend Patrick learned when he made the "complete stranger" comment. There are things better left unsaid.

These were the trivial events of November 1961. The year had started off well enough. In January, John Fitzgerald Kennedy was sworn in as America's

35th president. John Kennedy was an Irishman and a Roman Catholic. Sister Donovan and all the rest of us shared in his election victory, which clearly had resulted from our prayers.

I still feel badly about not paying attention to the old soldiers explaining what they had endured on my behalf.

December 2018

Come all ye weary media consumers—where seldom is heard an encouraging word—and just for a few minutes set aside reports of economic distress, political acrimony, social discontent, climate adjustment, cultural turbulence, fires, earthquakes, civil unrest, and the winter parking ban.

Instead, focus briefly on a few disparate scraps of not-so-bad local news from the last month of 2018—nothing much, just trivial, unrelated morsels of optimism, unserious stocking stuffers. Let nothing you dismay:

So far this winter, there's not much snow to speak of, the tyranny of Christmas shopping has come and gone, and the days are lengthening. New Year's Day in Nova Scotia is about forty-eight seconds longer than the previous day in terms of sunlight, allowing additional daylight for recovery from the seediness and infirmity contracted from celebrations on the previous night.

And there's good news for the men who were recently wandering aimlessly through the shopping malls, confused about what to get their wives for Christmas. It turns out that a few towering intellects (and some of the Scrooges I know) have determined that spouses are most grateful for inexpensive homemade gifts (given with genuine goodwill and affection), as opposed to costly presents contaminated by extravagance.

I think there's truth to it. This year, I was very pleased with the Newfoundland trigger mittens my wife knitted me, so I made her some festive snacks that included BBQ chips, Cape Breton crackers, and a cheeseball in the shape of Mike Duffy.

And who could complain about a gift as thoughtful as a hand-crafted Trudeau-in-India doll made from the cardboard tube left from the paper towel, or a homemade pepper grinder exactly the same size and shape as Gary

Burrill? For seniors, whose needs are modest, the possibilities of DIY gifting are unlimited.

And there's even more sunniness for the elderly. In December, the SHIFT (a demographic shift) report published by the government of Nova Scotia promised to validate and support the contributions of seniors. But it turns out we're not seniors; we're older adults whose diverse contributions are newly valued.

Apparently, some Nova Scotians think the term "seniors" damages our identity and contributes to the ageist stereotype that getting older is a problem. (I can only speak for myself, and I'm certainly not complaining, but I can assure the authors that, as a matter of fact, getting old *can* be a problem. Without getting into details, let's just say you can go for a long time when nothing much happens, and one day your age slaps you on the face.)

The introductory section of the SHIFT report suggests that the depravity of ageism manifests in comments like "I'm having a senior moment" or "You look good for your age." This is instructive. Clearly, I've missed opportunities to be offended, but I'll be more vigilant from now on. The same section also offers the insight that getting older is a natural part of life. Who knew?

In addition to the SHIFT report, Nova Scotia's older adults can take heart and inspiration from the recent announcement that a skinny seventy-five-year-old man trying to make a name for himself in the music industry will be touring throughout North America, beginning in the spring of 2019.

Mick Jagger, playing stadium concerts with his band members (with an average age of seventy-four), could never be accused of a sedentary lifestyle. Jagger's longevity as a performer may not be the result of clean living. This is encouraging for me and several people I am acquainted with. Mick, along with his fellow pensioners, provides counter-evidence that moderation is the answer. These old boys just keep moving—rolling stones gathering no moss.

And for those Haligonians looking for something to do after work, the atavistic impulse to throw axes is in fashion. In the New Year, an additional axe-throwing venue—just like darts, but with axes—will be opening on Brunswick Street where the owner promises a powerful social experience. There will be axe-throwing lanes available for team building, birthday parties, and meetings of the Public Accounts Committee. There is no truth to the rumour that the Liberals are planning to install axe-throwing corridors at the legislature––just gossip, someone with an axe to grind.

Post-secondary education will be improved in January when students attending the Ivany Campus of the NSCC will stay awake longer, possibly for the entire class, when a full-service Tim Hortons is installed on campus. Just across the street, the Dartmouth General Hospital lost its Tim Hortons earlier, when food choices were restricted at several Nova Scotia Health Authority sites. Apparently the Department of Education is okay with it.

And beer drinkers can rest easy knowing that none of the prolific local craft brewers use a recipe that includes romaine lettuce. Although projections indicate food costs will increase significantly next year, if you think beef is getting expensive, consider the cost of shooting moose from a helicopter in Cape Breton. Apparently, the cull costs the taxpayer about $8,000 per animal, which makes $4.99 a pound for ground beef (extra lean) seem like a bargain.

This year, one shopper complained that Christmas turkeys cost a lot more, causing some unexpected budgetary pain and suffering. Maybe so, but in my view, the turkey experience is worth the pain—and besides, no harm, no fowl.

For those thinking about having lobster on New Year's Day, more data is needed. According to a December *Chronicle Herald* article, lobsters (previously neglected in the social justice wars) were defended by PETA advocates with a large roadside poster on Barrington Street. They were speaking on behalf of the lobster pictured there—a message that the lobster would deliver itself, if only it could speak. "I am not meat," the sign said, which, among those of us who have been enjoying them for years, rings true enough. Only about twenty percent (by weight) is meat, and the rest (I'm told) is a substance called chitin which forms the exoskeleton. Also in the same article, a local lobster fisherman explains that lobsters have no central nervous system and no personality—which is bad news for lobsters because this means we cannot rule out the possibility that their species is related to government ministers or insurance salesmen.

In December, we learned that the first ever franchise of Gordonstoun, one of the world's most elite private schools, will soon be located somewhere in Annapolis County. The original Gordonstoun, located in Northern Scotland near Elgin, educated affluent young men, including Prince Philip and his princely sons Charles, Andrew, and Edward. (Gordonstoun is only a few miles east of Culloden, where another Bonnie Prince learned a valuable lesson in 1746.)

Soon, in Nova Scotia, grades nine through twelve will be available to students from around the world for a modest annual tuition fee of about $67,000—only about half of Adrienne Clarkson's expense account.

And in sporting news, media reports indicate that baseball fans (like me) have reason to be optimistic that Major League Baseball may soon return to Montreal. Having the Expos back is great news for old baseball enthusiasts who followed them since Charles Bronfman founded the team in 1968. Fifty years ago, some of us were lucky enough to see Rusty Staub and Maury Wills play in Jarry Park before the Olympic Stadium debacle.

And CFL football may be coming to HRM. Someone decided that the team will be called the Schooners, ignoring suggestions such as Resource-Hungry Roughriders or Taxpayers' Titans. Not to worry, all will be well.

Of course, there are many more serious reasons to be hopeful.

About being an optimist, it was Churchill who said *there's not much use being anything else.* My father had the best advice related to faith and confidence. He'd look up at the steeple of the old church in our parish and point out that although the parish priest had installed a large cross at the top, he put a lightning rod right beside it. Have faith, he advised—but hedge your bets.

Eclipsing the Moon

Late on a Sunday night, on the twentieth of January in 2019, we have something to look up to.

With an accuracy and precision that always amazes, astronomers are able to tell us with certainty that around midnight (it takes a while), the shadow of the Earth will darken a full moon, and we will enjoy the spectacle of a lunar eclipse if the skies are clear.

I am willing to take their word for it. I'm going to take a nap in the afternoon so I can stay up and enjoy it. These scientists have done a good job so far with celestial predictions and seem to be more reliable than erudite economists or political pundits. Since Copernicus defied Catholic doctrine and told us about the centre of our universe, even old skeptics like me tend to trust the star watchers.

I know almost nothing about space science, and my interest in the moon has waxed and waned over the years. These days, I look up at the night sky only rarely, usually to see lightning, fireworks, or airplane lights. When I was young—and the nights were quieter, colder, and darker—I would intermittently go outside on a clear night and spend some time gazing upwards, hoping to identify various constellations and planets, or maybe spot a shooting star, a UFO, or Batman.

Lately, I can only find the Big Dipper and North Star, but years ago, I went through a phase when I could accurately name the progression of moons in the night sky (new moons, quarters, waning crescents, waxing gibbous, full moons, etc.). I especially liked the evocative names for the full moons in the fall—the harvest moon, the hunter's moon, the beaver moon, the cold moon. Only once in a blue moon would I see two full moons in the same calendar month.

In 1969, when Neil Armstrong took those giant steps on the moon's surface—watching it on TV, my mother said he was light on his feet for such a big man—the world paid a lot more attention to lunar matters, but not much happened there since. That is, until earlier this month (January 2), when the Chinese went over to the dark side and landed a spacecraft on the lunar surface. No one except Pink Floyd has ever seen the dark side of the moon.

I hope the Chinese have sparked a renewed interest because these days (maybe speaking only for myself), I'm worried that the moon doesn't get the respect and attention it deserves. Now that we are photographing more distant planets (we're busy with Venus and Mars to see where men and women come from), it seems the moon has fallen out of fashion, with not many prospects on the horizon. Even the Man in the Moon, the imaginative tradition that recognizes a human in the image of a full moon, and which (even if we think it's kinda goofy) Stompin' Tom Connors has determined to be the face of a Newfie, is largely forgotten.

In any case, we would do well to remember that although its face is pockmarked and cratered, and its light borrowed from the sun, the moon has served us well and has earned our esteem.

Throughout history, the full moon on a cloudless night has been assigned onerous duties, responsible for poetic inspiration (The Moon was but a Chin of Gold), romanticizing courtship (it's lucky that moon rhymes with swoon), and lighting the midnight path of weary travelers.

Regrettably, it is unjustly associated with insanity and mental disorders which, at one time, were thought to be caused by a particular alignment of the moon and the planets. Lunacy (once suffered by those who were moonstruck) is now an antiquated designation, but was, during much of the nineteenth and twentieth centuries, a commonly used legal term.

In 2012, then President Barack Obama signed legislation removing the word "lunatic" from all federal laws in the U.S. Notwithstanding, experienced school teachers know about the influence of the full moon.

And then, there's "the tide in the affairs of men," for which the moon is responsible and which, "taken at the flood, leads on to fortune … and if omitted … life is bound in shallows and in miseries."

This is a big responsibility for the moon, whose gravitational pull is also accountable for the personality of the Bay of Fundy where tides are by their nature very egalitarian—a democratic moon-caused tide, raising all boats to the same level, not just those in Halls Harbour.

During the lunar eclipse, when the moon enters the Earth's shadow, it turns a rusty red colour, thus the blood moon. Citing biblical passages, some pessimistic prognosticators suggest the blood moon signals that the end of the world will occur in the days following. This is an unfavourable consequence, and could interfere with the Super Bowl and those planning to travel south later in the month.

As impressive as the moon is, its celebrity will be eclipsed by the Earth's shadow on Sunday—check it out; if you don't stay up to see it, you'll have to wait until 2021.

The Two-Faced Season

During this first month of the calendar year, it is not surprising that we have the agreeable habit of looking forward (resolutions, projections, predictions, first babies) and backward (year-end reviews, highlights, achievements, disasters) at the same time.

The month of January is, of course, named after Janus, the ancient Roman god of looking to the past and future, the god of beginnings and endings, the god of transitions, gates and doorways. Janus, presiding over the gates of Rome, looked with two faces in opposite directions, forward and backward. Janus perceived both with equal clarity.

In 1961 my grade five teacher could do the same thing. Sister Donovan, a relative of Janus (and allegedly a Sister of Charity) had eyes in both the front and back of her head. The pair in the back was hidden by a black veil, but it was obvious they could see right through it.

While she was facing the blackboard writing today's lesson in longhand, she was able, with no apparent effort, to detect and correct the aberrant behaviour of the twelve-year-old boys behind her: *Patrick, sit up straight; Tommy, turn around in your seat; William, bring that note you're passing and put it on my desk so we can all enjoy it.*

These rear-view admonitions did not in any way interrupt or interfere with the work in front of Sister Donovan. She could remedy miscreant conduct while filling the entire blackboard with perfect precision and perfect penmanship, as if she were an ancient scribe copying the Torah.

Sister Donovan believed in God, cleanliness, the rule of law, and neatness. She reverentially referred to the virtue of penmanship as if it had had the same rank and standing as citizenship or stewardship. In her domain, the meaning of words was secondary to their appearance.

After returning from the Christmas holiday in January 1961, Sister Janus-Donovan was explaining to us that this particular New Year had unique significance because its digits looked the same when it was written upside down. I'm not sure why she attributed any importance to this odd fact, but she seemed to feel it had some religious implications. She explained that the last time it happened was almost 200 years before in 1881 (when both U.S. President James Garfield and Billy the Kid were killed) and challenged us to discover the next year when this mysterious numerical inversion would occur (I think we have to wait about 4,000 years until 6009, but I'm still not sure). Sister Donovan was baptized with lemon juice, but she did have some interesting morsels from time to time.

At the time Sister Donovan was going on about turning numbers upside down, my Uncle Joseph (who lived well out in the suburbs of Sister Donovan's spiritual world) developed some questionable theories about the final year of each decade, especially the years of the twentieth century that ended with the digit 9. He contended (perhaps unseriously) that these years included a disproportionate amount of historical activity, as if each decade was trying to squeeze as much commotion as possible into the last year before a new decade begins.

QUESTIONABLE COMMENTARY

He updated the evidence annually, until about twenty years ago. Samples of Uncle Joe's miscellaneous evidence included:

> *In 1919, the Treaty of Versailles was signed, Einstein confirmed the Theory of Relativity, Ernest Rutherford split the atom, Charles Strite invented the pop-up toaster, the Boston Red Sox traded Babe Ruth, and the Chicago White Sox fixed the World Series.*

> *In 1929, the stock market collapsed and the Great Depression began.*

> *In 1939, the Second World War began and the Spanish Civil War ended.*

> *In 1949, Ireland became a republic, the Soviet Union tested an atomic bomb, the People's Republic of China was proclaimed.*

> *In 1959, Fidel Castro came to power in Cuba and the FLQ bombed the stock exchange in Montreal.*

> *In 1969, the first man walked on the moon, the Woodstock Music Festival was happening, and the Troubles began in Ireland.*

> *In 1979, the Islamic Revolution was underway in Iran and McDonald's introduced the Happy Meal.*

> *In 1989, communism in Eastern Europe collapsed, the Berlin Wall was dismantled, and scenes from Tiananmen Square were broadcast around the world.*

> *In 1999, Wayne Gretzky retired from hockey.*

Joe's dubious end-of-the-decade cramming-it-in theory seems a bit silly, but Joe was a smart guy and this is how I remember it. (Uncle Joe is dead now and can't chirp in.) We'll see how it works out for 2019.

My wife and I agree that we have had a good year. Our children and grandchildren are flourishing, we enjoy reasonably good health, we have great friends and neighbours, spring will be here soon enough, and the Blue Jays are strengthening their bullpen.

Looking backward to 2018, it seems to me we are fortunate in ways we don't even understand, and looking forward to 2019, everyone might consider Sister Donovan's advice: give what you can, take what comes, and God's mercy on us all.

Now, if Janus the god of passageways allows it, I'll journey down the hall to the kitchen and make a cup of tea.

OLD-SCHOOL STUFF

Molasses

One hundred years ago, on January 15, 1919, an explosion occurred in Boston during the lunchtime break at 529 Commercial Street. A steel storage tank fifty feet tall, two-hundred-and-forty-feet wide, and containing more than two million gallons of black molasses erupted, and its contents covered much of the north end of the city.

The explosion resulted in a wave of molasses twenty feet high, travelling thirty miles per hour, and powerful enough to lift a train off an elevated railway. The black surge destroyed a number of buildings, dozens of horses, killed twenty-one people and injured one hundred and fifty others. Most of the dead were poor Italian immigrants who populated the area where the molasses tank was situated.

Sixty years ago, on January 15, 1959, I was having breakfast with my father when he told me the story of the explosion. He seemed to know everything about it. It was bitter cold outside and we were sitting at the kitchen table filling up with pancakes. The pancakes were substantial, cooked by my mother on her griddle, a black chunk of cast iron weighing five hundred pounds with a crude handle; it covered most of the surface of our kitchen oil stove.

There were green Melmac plates on the table, a black plastic tube radio, and a messy container of Crosby's Molasses, also black. And there was a non-popup manual toaster which (unless monitored closely) produced burnt black toast. Black toast was not discarded; it was scraped, margarined, jammed, and eaten. The kitchen radio—the communications centre of our house—was tuned to CBC, and when the news was over that morning (Alaska had just been admitted as the forty-ninth state), it was followed by an advertisement for Dodd's Little Liver Pills.

The black AM radio was covered with bread crumbs because it sat beside the manual flip toaster near the back. My father exercised absolute jurisdiction over the radio. It was only used to hear the news and the weather. There was clearly no sense wearing it out with music or other indulgences.

QUESTIONABLE COMMENTARY

As I mentioned, the yellowed dial was always turned to CBC. It had a louvered speaker, two white knobs under the circular dial, and the outside was made from a miracle plastic called Bakelite. The tubes inside got very hot, distorted the Bakelite, burned out, and had to be replaced by sending it away. The radio was manufactured by Admiral, and the knobs, each with a stylized *A* in the middle, often came off and fell on the kitchen floor.

My father turned the radio down to tell me the molasses story.

At the time, my father was attentive to events in Boston, partly because of the Irish community there, but mostly because of Ted Williams and the Boston Red Sox. He reminded me that Boston was called Beantown precisely because of the lucrative molasses trade, and the expanding market for their locally produced baked beans—beans with molasses so tasty they came to be called Boston Baked Beans to distinguish them from other, less agreeable brands.

My father was a sober and temperate man, but on this morning he uncharacteristically (while marmalading a piece of burnt toast) tried to be funny by suggesting that when the deluge occurred, the deadly molasses forgot that, consistent with its reputation, it was supposed to move slowly. *Everybody knows that when molasses moves from one place to another, it takes its time.*

Yeah, I said, *especially in January.*

Unexpectedly, these comments made my father laugh out loud, a phenomenon which happened hardly at all. I didn't understand why he found it so funny, but my father's unrestrained laughing is the only reason I remember that breakfast and the molasses story. It was a long time ago.

At the time of the explosion, molasses was a valuable commodity. Commonly used to sweeten soft drinks, to produce ethyl alcohol (mostly rum), baked beans, and other everyday products, it was the standard sweetener of the day.

During the First World War, it was also a key component in the manufacture of munitions. The day after the Boston molasses tsunami, the U.S. Congress ratified the 18th Amendment to the United States Constitution which prohibited the manufacture, transport, and sale of all alcoholic beverages—a national prohibition that was possibly one of the most ill-conceived social experiments in American history.

I finished my pancakes and grabbed one of my mother's tea biscuits, split it in two, and applied a generous dollop of molasses on each. The molasses had the consistency of Bunker-C, and when I sat the container down on the table, the residue near the opening began drooling down the side, moving very slowly, behaving like it was supposed to. I watched its slow descent and caught it with my knife just before it hit the plastic tablecloth. My father had turned up the radio to hear the weather forecast. I finished the biscuit, licked my knife, and put my plate in the sink.

After Beantown was covered with molasses, the Bostonian Society honoured the victims of the explosion by erecting a plaque in the north end of the city near the entrance to Puopolo Park.

Now, a hundred years later, residents claim that if you walk near the park on a hot summer afternoon, you can still smell the molasses.

I'd like to think you can.

Loretta Leaks

In a recent newspaper column, a local journalist lamented the loss of decency and civility in the behaviour and daily discourse among those who live in a universe where folks interact at the safe and impersonal distances provided by technology.

I agree. Social media has provided no shortage of evidence of the demise of courtesy and the coarsening of our culture.

As an example of the way things used to be handled (face to face), the journalist recalls a rebuke from a freckle-faced girl (maybe fifty years ago) at Sir Charles Tupper School in Halifax.

The article dredged up another misty example of an early-school experience that demonstrates a civil and courteous response to an unfortunate classroom accident which happened even earlier than the rebuke from the red-haired girl.

It's not a particularly useful memory, but it is mildly entertaining and surprisingly durable. In 1956, when I was seven years old, Loretta Walker was my friend (even though she was a girl), and she peed her pants while she was sitting at her desk in our grade two classroom.

The appearance of that classroom, the dour nun standing at the blackboard, and Loretta's unfortunate accident contribute my only memories from grade two.

QUESTIONABLE COMMENTARY

I can give an accurate accounting because I was an eyewitness. I was sitting at the desk right behind Loretta, within arm's length. It was the last week of school before the summer vacation. Here's how it happened.

I went to a Catholic school where everything was old––the plumbing, the hardwood floors, the nuns––all decrepit. There was no evidence of renovation or maintenance (except light dusting) since the cornerstone was laid.

Our grade two classroom and its pious overseer were formidable in every aspect. Sister Aquinas was rendered in black and white, and the rest of the classroom was burnt sienna. The ceilings were twelve feet high and the tall windows facing the road opened from the top, discouraging escape. No one was allowed to touch those windows except the despotic nun who controlled them with a ten-foot pole; a metal hook at the end allowed her to pull down the rounded upper sashes. (If you looked out of any of these windows, you could see a sign next to the road, warning motorists to reduce speed. The sign said SLOW CHILDREN. It was designed for our safety, but threatened our self-esteem.)

The classroom door was massive, about four feet wide, made from thick, dense oak. It had a well-worn door knob, huge hinges and key plate, all of these cast from heavy-gage solid brass––enough to supply the British Admiralty.

Sister Aquinas was a hefty, solemn nun, at least nominally a Sister of Charity. This designation required her to shroud herself in voluminous multi-layered black drapery. The bottom portion revealed only the toes of her dark (sensible) shoes. Like a Texas border guard watching for illegal immigrants (Protestants), Aquinas patrolled the first-floor hallway.

She walked those halls in a long black veil. It covered her entire head except for her pious face, which was framed by a pure, white arc of corrugated cardboard, blinders whose construction was reminiscent of a small garden arch or a croquet wicket. This arch of corrugation seriously impaired Sister Aquinas's visual perceptions, apparently to both good and bad effect.

Because of it, she was unable to be distracted by the depravity and wickedness lurking on the edges of her vision. On the other hand, she would be disadvantaged had she decided on a career playing professional basketball where peripheral vision is essential.

Her outfit was further accessorized by a starched white bib in the front, useful if she was planning a feed of lobster. Sister Aquinas could move up and down the aisles without making any noise and without moving her feet. She was mounted on well-oiled castors. Sister Aquinas was ancient, and by the time we met her, all of the Christian charity had been emptied out of her. She couldn't be bought off with children's smiles.

Buried in the pleats and folds of the black material that was her habit, a portion of a great rosary dangled from some hidden bracket. Usually, one of Sister Aquinas's arms was buried in the dense, black fabric draped over her chest under the pristine bib. She could reach deep inside the pleats and folds of her frock and dig out almost anything—a box of tissue, a packet of Crayola, a fountain pen, a yardstick, a pink eraser, an elastic band, a handgun, a crucifix, the Old Testament, a framed photograph of the Pope Pius XII, the severed head of John the Baptist, or any textbook on the approved list. Had it been invented, she could easily have come up with an overhead projector.

All of the children's desk/chair assemblies were made from maple hardwood—ink-stained, gouged, chipped, and carved with initials and enigmatic symbols. The desks contained hardened gum, eraser crumbs, pencil shavings, decomposing fruit, and the bones of dead mice. The desk legs and the chair pedestals were made of indestructible cast iron that was smelted in a Bessemer furnace during the Industrial Revolution. All of the students' desks and chairs were in exactly the same position they had been since Jesus was a boy, permanently screwed to the hardwood floor. The screws were twisted and corroded and leaked rusty stains on the hardwood from which the varnish had worn many years earlier.

Because the desks had never moved, the children's feet that shuffled beneath them for more than half a century had worn depressions in the hardwood. There was a scooped-out area in the hardwood under every desk. These gave an unusual scalloped effect to the entire surface.

These floor depressions are central to the story of Loretta's misfortune, and her subsequent celebrity.

It was a warm day in the last week of June and Loretta was wearing black, plastic shoes. On this particular morning, with no warning or provocation, she peed her pants, generously and without intermission. Loretta appeared oblivious. She stoically carried on with her printing exercises while the effluent trickled down her legs and filled the hollow in the floor at her feet.

I became aware of this flooding just as her reservoir had reached its capacity. The overflow created a tributary heading in my direction. As the floor depression at my own feet was similarly filled, I spread my legs and put one foot on either shore. Theatrical straddling by me, and giggling from others, caught the attention of the Black Knight who was about to issue a reprimand but, glancing downward, quickly realized what was going on.

Sister Aquinas closed her eyes, blessed herself, said a Hail Mary, and sprang into action. Incontinent Loretta was removed from among us—nobody knows where she went. No fuss was made, and the puddles were cleaned up by Mr. O'Leary, the school's janitor.

Loretta resurfaced the next day and acted as if nothing had happened, as did we all. It was all quite seamless. In our school, there were only two rules: Mind your Manners and Don't Make a Fuss. And Sit Up Straight and Tuck in Your Shirt. That's four rules already, and there were a whole lot more.

In the text of Ulysses, James Joyce claimed that it was a nun who invented barbed wire. Although he didn't mention Sister Aquinas by name, I'm pretty sure she was the one.

It ended well. No fuss was made. Loretta's shoes were made of plastic, and the following week school was over for the summer. No electronic record of the event exists.

Pencils Reconsidered

Last night I watched a courtroom scene on television where an elderly lawyer, holding a yellow legal pad, was sitting quietly listening to the proceedings and using a pencil to take copious notes. It was the pencil that caught my attention. It seemed anachronistic. Pencils are endangered in recent days. It seems they have fallen from fashion (unless you're a carpenter, or an artist, or a prime-time lawyer).

When I was in elementary school in the 1950s (the middle ages), every kid carried a pencil case. It was standard equipment, mandated by statute and by the nun at the front of the room. Every pencil case contained the following items: two or more sharpened HB pencils (two was the mandatory minimum), a single pink eraser, a pencil sharpener, and a mess of pencil shavings (the detritus of the sharpening). The sharpener, usually red, could be a one-holer or a two-holer.

Although the pencils were of various lengths (stages of their life), they were always yellow with teeth marks, and stamped HB (hard and black). The eraser that was found on the end of new pencils was usually chewed off (some of the antiestablishment kids broke off the eraser part and sharpened both ends). Students needed an eraser (the Pink Pearl) because during that era there was less concern for self-esteem––children got at least as many things wrong as they got right. On every Pink Pearl, the original beveled edge was worn round.

Thoughtfully, the nuns decreed no upper limit on the number of allowed pencils. The girls usually carried an inventory that caused the sides of their case to bulge and made it hard to close the zipper. The aristocratic girls had coloured pencils and a fountain pen (Waterman).

At the beginning of the school day, the pencil case contained a nickel because that was the cost of the fresh milk delivered to our classroom at recess, in a small glass bottle with a cardboard top and a little tab you could lift to insert a straw. It was the age of miracle and wonder.

By the time we got to grade five, the nuns lifted the pencil case requirement and only girls and wimpy boys carried one. The sophisticated boys kept pencils in their pockets, where they were lost or broken. If ever one was needed, it could be borrowed from one of the girls.

When I was in grade five, one particular pencil contributed to the callous and painful skewering of Margaret O'Connell, a fine, fleshy girl with big ears and a head like a sugar bowl. Margaret was impaled by my best friend, an eager boy named Patrick McGinn, known only by his last name.

McGinn had a new HB pencil he was proud of. The eraser was intact and the yellow paint was pristine, hardly any teeth-marks at all. He sharpened his new pencil to a needlepoint while Margaret (who sat in front of him) was out of her seat to retrieve a dog-eared dictionary from the teacher's desk.

McGinn had an idea that when Margaret sat back down, he would lean forward and touch the tip of his new pencil lightly to her butt, with the intention of a minor pinch producing a squeal that would get her in trouble and not him. This turned out to be a bad idea.

Without realizing it, McGinn positioned the non-slip eraser end of the pencil against the wooden seat perpendicular to Margaret's meaty buttocks. When Margaret went to sit down, she did not suddenly jump up as McGinn had calculated. Instead she fell heavily into her seat, turned white and let out a blood-curdling scream that could be heard to the city limits. It may have startled pigeons on downtown buildings, loosened fillings, or derailed a train.

There was only one place for the pencil to go. Margaret was near death and inconsolable.

Sister Donovan (her face contorted and white) blessed herself as she passed in front of the statue of The Virgin. Then she shit her pants and said *Mother of God, intercede for us all.* She helped Margaret struggle to her feet, allowing the rest of us a full view of the impalement. About half of the seven-inch pencil was buried in her backside. Margaret continued screaming without interruption. To demonstrate their willingness to help, all the other girls in the class screeched and bawled in sympathy. Teachers from adjacent classrooms appeared at our door, visibly shaken. The most virtuous girl in our class (known to us as Our Lady Kathleen) declared a state of emergency, drew on her vast reservoir of goodness, and repaired to the end of the hall to retrieve the principal. Sister Donovan assumed the demeanor of Mother Teresa caring for the wounded and the dying.

Two teachers carried Margaret, each lifting an arm, from the classroom. It was a memorable scene. Margaret looked like she had been shot with a crossbow while retreating from a medieval castle. There was no getting around it–– Margaret had a pencil in her arse.

Left alone in the classroom for a few minutes, we wondered aloud if Margaret would survive; would Father Dolan show up to anoint her head with oil? Would rigor mortis set in? And what about the funeral, would we get a day off school?

Margaret was taken to the teacher's room where (we later learned) the pencil was vigorously removed by Sister Donovan. We didn't see what happened in the teacher's room, but later we reported it to others as if we had been there. Over the next few days and weeks, the impalement and the extraction became legend, described in great detail–– Sister Donovan, with one foot on the floor and the other on Margaret's ass, grunting as she pulled on the pencil with both hands, falling backward when it came loose, picking herself up to rinse the bloody pencil under the tap, and then pulling down Margaret's pants to sterilize the wound with a mercurochrome.

In memory, the most vivid aspect of the incident was Margaret's piercing scream. (We never heard anything like it again until grade nine, when Danny Dalton got his scrotum caught in a filing cabinet drawer). Both Margaret and

McGinn missed a few days of school. It was never clear what happened while they were gone——Margaret, presumably for medical attention, McGinn to the Gulag for solitary confinement or (we imagined) lethal injection. But after a few days, both returned and daily routines were restored. No fuss was made. For a period of time, Margaret sat on a foam cushion. McGinn asked Sister Donovan if he could get his pencil back. The reception for his request was unfavourable.

Notwithstanding Margaret's misfortune, I think the noble pencil should be born again. We should embrace its all-natural materials (no chemicals, no plastic). Discard the Fine-point, the Sharpie, and the Rollerball. Sharpen our wits. Get the lead out.

Mrs. Gannet's Grammar

Because of my non-participation, I really have no business commenting on (or writing about) matters related to social-media communications.

However, I'm not deterred. If I were to restrict myself only to areas of expertise, well, the problem is obvious. I am not involved with Bookface, Twitter, or the various species of messaging, but I now have an iPhone which I can use to send and receive emails and texts. This development has conferred on me far more status and technological sophistication than I was allocated previously.

Lately, I've been reading about folks concerned about the impact of social-media messaging on the old-fashioned business of spelling, punctuation, and grammatical precision. Some free-thinking advocates suggest that shorthand messaging accounts for almost all of the writing people do these days, and writing practice of any kind is a good thing. It allows scribblers, young and old, to innovate, experiment, and sharpen their skills constantly——about every three and a half minutes.

Some of these towering intellects suggest that we shouldn't bother ourselves with the conventions of language——capitalization is preventable, grammar is for the elderly, and ending a sentence with a period can be a bit judgmental.

Others believe that the truncated and flawed language of text messages (along with emojis, emoticons, hashtags, etc.) is eroding the value of writing the world over. These folks feel anxious about the social acceptance (even encouragement) of shorthand expression, and they are apprehensive about articulating the nuances of expression in one hundred and forty characters or less.

Some perceive such shorthand habits as a form of pollution that assigns spelling and grammar to the endangered species list––and may forecast the end of civilization.

I don't know if current trends (tweets, emojis, hashtags, autocorrect, etc.) are an aid to literary composition or if they indicate the sad demise of decent writing, but while recently contemplating the whole social-media debate, I recalled (with surprising clarity) experiences with an ancient and influential high school teacher.

Years ago Mrs. Gannet taught us English grammar (in grade twelve) during the Neolithic period––the era of oil stoves, ringer washers, mothballs, and car-tire chains. When people fixed things instead of throwing them out, doctors made house calls, people shined their shoes, schoolchildren kept notes with a pencil, and hash was made from corned beef and potatoes.

Back then, our high school was not yet attentive to the virtues of a holistic approach to language development. English literature was taught separately from English grammar. In grade twelve, I was in an English class that was designated "Enhanced."

Some students were selected for this group because they were the best and the brightest. The rest of us were chosen because we *showed promise,* an expression of optimism necessary to provide gender balance because the best language students were almost exclusively girls.

We (who *showed promise*) were underachievers not performing up to our potential. Underachievers had special status (we imagined) because this designation implied untapped genius. We were handpicked for poor performance. We had cunningly established a baseline low enough to allow for more growth than the elite group who made the mistake of operating too close to their ceiling of excellence. We had outfoxed them.

As a result, I ended up in Mrs. Gannet's class. She was an elderly, sedate lady, tall and skinny with features like a tropical bird: a thin beak, short grey hair feathered back on the sides, and hollow bones, strong but light if she wanted to take flight.

She walked in short steps and had a facility with words that was neither affected nor ostentatious, and we enjoyed listening to her talk. When she was at the front of the classroom, everybody listened.

She always carried a wad of Kleenex to dab the end of her drippy beak. When the tissue wasn't in her hand, she balled it up and shoved it up the sleeve of her sweater, making a conspicuous tumor on her hollow, blue-veined arm. Sometimes she stood on one leg.

Mrs. Gannet valued parsing sentences and conjugating verbs, as well as lengthy and obscure words. In September, when she pointed out the difference between sin tax (a levy on cigarettes and alcohol) and syntax (an understanding of which she hoped to pass along to us), I knew we were going to be friends.

For a while in September, I thought Mrs. Gannet was confused about various articulations. She pronounced the "r" in February and the "n" in Wednesday. She thought the day after Monday was *Chewsday*, and the Queen's husband the *Jook of Edinburgh*.

Mrs. Gannet lamented the decline of the King's English and saw herself as a missionary doing God's work, inculcating grammatical virtue. Good manners and good grammar, she said, were equally necessary to repair the crumbling foundations of propriety. (I have since read that the rise of evangelical religions and burgeoning lotto-ticket sales are indicators of the failing health of a nation; Mrs. Gannet's world order held that poor grammar and faulty punctuation provided the evidence of civilization collapsing.)

In particular, the girls in our class admired the aristocratic Mrs. Gannet. They saw her as an intelligent, refined lady with deportment worthy of emulation. One girl in particular, a red-haired girl named Kathleen, was an irritating high-achiever prone to melodrama, with an obsequious temperament. Not happy with having the top marks in the class, Kathleen constantly sought Gannet's approval and courted her favour. Kathleen radiated an air of rectitude. This did not endear her to the rest of us. We called her *The Divinity*.

It was a good day when *The Divinity* suggested to Mrs. Gannet that they shared a mutual interest in the English language. Kindly, Mrs. Gannet used the opportunity to explain Kathleen's error. *Oh no,* she said, *we do not have a mutual interest in language, but rather a common interest. Mutual,* she explained, *requires reciprocity––two people can have a mutual interest in each other. If they both have an interest in something else, it is a common interest.*

Kathleen's freckled face turned red. Good enough for her. Witnessing embarrassment long overdue brings people together. It proved God's existence. The

Divinity had been corrected, amended in her area of expertise, vanquished on her own turf, hoisted with her own petard.

Exchanging smiles and glances, we commoners tried not to show how pleased we were. The Germans call it *schadenfreude*.

Mrs. Gannet was unaffected and quickly segued to the next topic, the evils of misplaced modifiers and dangling participles.

On another occasion, I can remember Mrs. Gannet sitting (roosting) on a stool in the corner, while students went to the front of the room to read their compositions. She was insessorial *(adjective: relating to birds that perch or are adapted for perching)* while taking notes.

I can recall vividly my friend Patrick reading aloud (with indifference) in front of the class with his pant leg tucked into his sock (he rode his bicycle to school) and his fly down. Watching with equanimity, Mrs. Gannet listened attentively, and when Pat was done reading, she explained to him that *irregardless* was not a word, and then she said his story (Techniques of Tire Repair) was *surprisingly good*. She didn't mention his zipper.

In her ancient, orderly world, Mrs. Gannet valued new technologies such as the Waterman fountain pen and the Gutenberg Press, but I'm pretty sure she would reject the current conventions associated with social media.

If I imagine her writing anything omitting punctuation or capital letters, or using an emoticon, or sending a tweet, it makes me LOL.

Learning by Heart

At one time, we had a prime minister who wore a rose in his lapel, pirouetted for the Queen, practiced yoga, earned a brown belt in judo, and explained to the press that he frequently stood on his head.

In 1981, not long after his inauguration, President Ronald Reagan visited Pierre Trudeau in Ottawa and had a conversation with his ten-year-old son Justin. Reagan asked young Justin if he was interested in stories from the Old West, and (after being assured that he was) Reagan proceeded to recite, from memory, a poem by Robert Service: *The Shooting of Dan McGrew*.

Our current prime minister claims he was so impressed with the recitation that he later memorized the poem himself.

A neighbour, friend, and fellow retiree of my vintage is a kindred spirit to poets like Willie Nelson and Robert Service, and occasionally enjoys reciting aloud a few lines from Willie's classic *Roll Me Up & Smoke Me When I Die*, or Robert Service's *The Cremation of Sam McGee*.

Usually, spontaneous recitations like these occur in the evening while we are enjoying a glass of Bushmills' *Uisce Beatha* — in Irish Gaelic, "the water of life." We also know a couple of stanzas of *The Ballad of Dan McGrew*, and miscellaneous other bits and pieces of verse, including *Invictus* by William Henley whose head remains *bloody but unbowed*.

These and other half-remembered snippets of doggerel come up from time to time. It pleases us that we can remember them. Older adults who can't recall what they had for breakfast that morning take comfort in remembering stuff they learned when they were young.

I was in grade ten when Mr. MacPherson, upholstered in tweed and flannel, taught us manners and Canadian history. That year (1965), a red and white maple leaf design was proclaimed the new flag of Canada. MacPherson, a man with a head like a russet potato and a true patriot, thumbtacked the new flag to the front wall above the blackboard.

MacPherson was a wonderful teacher who taught with conviction Canada's role in The Great War and the horrors of trench warfare in Belgium and France. His favourite war poet was Wilfred Owen, who wrote compelling descriptions of the revulsions of the First World War gas attacks.

I vividly remember a day in November when MacPherson stood before the new flag to recite from memory, with tears in his eyes, Owen's poem *Dulce et Decorum Est*. MacPherson remembered the words with his head, but delivered them from his heart—by heart.

His uncle had been killed at Vimy Ridge, and if any of us wanted to get a credit in his course, we had to memorize "In Flanders Fields" and (before the final exam) stand beside his desk and recite it flawlessly, and with expression.

MacPherson's world view included the belief that some material should be committed to memory. This commitment was a civic duty and necessary for the preservation of democracy.

My wife, Yvonne, likes to tell a story about an incident that happened in Cape Breton about fifty-five years ago. As a child, she was being driven from

Antigonish by her Uncle Remi, a serious and thoughtful man, on a beautiful summer evening, to her home in Margaree.

He was chauffeuring along silently as darkness crept into the lovely Margaree Valley. Moved by the venue, Uncle Remi, without preamble, spoke aloud the first couple of lines of a Longfellow poem: *The day is done, and the darkness falls from the wings of night.*

Before Remi could continue, Yvonne (then age ten) chirped in and completed the stanza, *As a feather is wafted downward from an eagle in his flight.*

Remi was delighted. He let it be known that he was proud and pleased that she was able to complete the passage. Yvonne will always remember her uncle's poignant response. It made her feel clever, adult, and part of some undefined community of poets. Today she can still recite Longfellow's poem by heart (along with passages from many more), but the pride she felt at the time is the sentiment that has endured.

Our generation went to school during a period when memorizing was not considered a deterrent to learning. Memorization was esteemed, and in some classrooms, mandated by statute. Learning stuff by heart was held in high regard.

Not just poetry. At various times, we memorized a boatload of other stuff: The multiplication tables, the Baltimore Catechism, Latin verb conjugations, the major rivers of Canada, the provincial flowers, the Ten Commandments, the order of the planets, the monarchs of England, the dates of major wars, the periodic table, the speed of acceleration due to gravity, the number of feet in a mile, the first twenty-five prime numbers, the first ten prime ministers, the inventor of the cotton gin, the speed of light, the law of cosines, the effects of the Industrial Revolution, the phases of the moon, the stages of a butterfly's development, the capital of Manitoba, Linnaeus's taxonomy, the quadratic formula, and Pi to six places past the decimal.

And every year, we had to memorize a few poems and stand at the front of the room and recite them––*with expression*. Reciting with expression was well-regarded. It indicated an interest in what you were saying. Surprisingly, most of our generation that was required to memorize poetry in high school (they've forgotten the drudgery of learning them and the nervousness of reciting them) will happily recommend it, and are pleased to demonstrate how much they can still recall.

I'm talking about the recollections of the general population of retirees who survived the chore of rote learning (not academic deep thinkers who imagine they know more about a poem's meaning than the poet) and feel good about it.

Among our group, probably sixty-five or older, everyone has their own examples of entire poems, half-remembered snippets, miscellaneous passages, lines and titles (the list is endless) which they can recall, or partially recall, or claim to recall—a list that may include words from geniuses such as these:

> Frost: *I have promises to keep and miles to go before I sleep.*
>
> Kilmer: *I think that I will never see a poem as lovely as a tree.*
>
> Dickinson: *Because I could not stop for death, he kindly stopped for me.*
>
> Coleridge: *In Xanadu did Kubla Khan a stately pleasure dome decree.*
>
> Noyes: *The road was a ribbon of moonlight over the purple moor.*
>
> Yeats: *I will arise and go now, and go to Innisfree.*
>
> Eliot: *April is the cruelest month.*
>
> Thomas: *Rage against the dying of the light.*
>
> Thayer: *Mighty Casey has struck out.*
>
> Magee: *I have slipped the surly bonds of earth.*
>
> Service: *There are strange things done in the midnight sun.*
>
> Tennyson: *He clasps the crag with crooked hands.*
>
> Shakespeare: *Shall I compare thee to a summer's day?*
>
> Browning: *Grow old along with me.*
>
> Donne: *Never send to know for whom the bell tolls, it tolls for thee*
>
> … And many, many more.

Among us non-serious rote learners of poetry, maybe the most memorable were the doggerel scribblers like Ogden Nash who was my favourite. He could disparage the Scottish in five words (*No McTavish was ever lavish*) or describe a cow (*The cow is of the bovine ilk; One end is moo, the other, milk*) or provide advice about eating celery (*Celery raw, develops the jaw, but celery stewed, is more quietly chewed*).

Years ago, the tradition of memorization did not survive the assault of progressive educational theorists who imagined rote learning as an oppressive act (*constructivism*, in particular, was hostile) and when Benjamin Bloom published his enduring taxonomy of educational objectives, he assigned knowledge (remembering stuff) to the lowest level.

Bloom's hierarchy, emphasizing the importance of critical thinking, analyzing and synthesizing information, seems reasonable enough—sort of—and currently, the business of remembering is assigned to Siri, Alexa and Associates.

But there was a time when poetry—memorized, recited poetry—was revered.

It may be an affliction of old age to advocate for past practice, but maybe Ogden Nash was right when he suggested "progress may have been alright at one time, but it has gone on way too long."

(In 1965 when MacPherson was teaching us about the war, my father bought a 78 RPM record of Pierre Berton reciting the poems of Robert Service. Money was tight in those days; purchasing recorded poetry strains the imagination.)

Back to today. Just a few doors down the street I have a friend who is an eminent and successful professional, a principal in a prominent engineering firm and a surprisingly wise man, properly concerned with the tensions and compressions of the world.

John is a proud lowland Scot (his family immigrated to Nova Scotia from Dumfriesshire) who claims a practical and pragmatic common-sense world view in the tradition of Thomas Reid, James Wilson, and the other Common-Sense Men of the eighteenth century Scottish Enlightenment. A man of science and logic, John purports not much use for the distractions of romantic literature or the watery sentiments of writers and poets.

But here's the thing. After a *wee deoch an' doris* (just a wee drop, that's all) of *Laphroaig* (Islay single malt, from the Inner Hebrides), John can be counted on to mutate into an armchair philosopher, and there's a good chance he will spontaneously begin to recite some scandalous Scottish doggerel or other entertaining verse, some of it printable, some not.

He delivers it with expression, with enthusiasm, and with a Scottish burr.

Never mind Thomas Telford, James Watt, John McAdam, and the other Scottish titans of science and industry; I see more evidence of Robbie Burns and Walter Scott than he imagines.

Funny thing, that.

Chocolate Maps and Pointy Sticks

If anyone my age begins a conversation with the words "back when I went to school," they should note their audience's response: The younger people (those under 50) will glance furtively at each other, eyes will roll, eyebrows will elevate. Some may mutter under their breath or remain silent with disparaging thoughts like *here we go again....sure, everything was better in the good-old-days....teachers taught and students listened...back in the day...there was respect and discipline....* I've heard it all before...

Back when I went to school we studied geography. Geography had status. I could be wrong but it seems that the education of children these days does not include the same emphasis on geography as it once did. If this is true, maybe it should be remediated.

In 2011, in conversation with Governor Arnold Schwarzenegger, Canada's (then) Minister of Defense Peter MacKay claimed that California and British Columbia shared a common border, forgetting briefly that both Washington and Oregon separate them somewhat. During a campaign stop in 2008, presidential candidate Barak Obama claimed he had visited fifty-seven states. The current American President recently revealed he doesn't know the difference between England and Great Britain. And a 2014 survey by the National Science Foundation discovered that twenty-five percent of Americans don't know the earth revolves around the sun.

Notwithstanding these deficits, geography holds an innate interest for most people. We all like to know where on this planet we are situated and are naturally inquisitive about the location of others. This curiosity shows itself in a variety of ways. (Recently, many of us had to google––or grab the atlas––when we heard about the tragic events in West Africa, in Burkina Faso).

Back when I went to school, in grades seven to nine we had a geography class every day. There were no computers, smartboards, or smart phones—only smart alecks. What we did have was two huge maps, one of Canada and one of the World. All the kids called them the "chocolate-bar maps." Everyone over sixty-five who went to school in Atlantic Canada knows what I'm talking about.

They hung conspicuously in every classroom, supplied free to all schools by William Neilson Limited, maker of Neilson's Chocolate Bars. The maps were about four feet tall and five feet wide with a sturdy wooden stick at the top and bottom, allowing the maps to be rolled up and tied with a red ribbon if the blackboard space behind them was needed. There was a picture of a chocolate bar in every corner, which I later learned the teacher was not allowed to conceal because the maps were provided free to schools only if they agreed not to hide the advertisements. The unobstructed display of candy was part of the covenant between Neilson and the public school system, linking sugar and cocoa beans to social studies and civic duty. In my experience there were only two versions of the chocolate bar maps, one labelled "Canada" and the other labelled "The World". At the time the World map was dominated by the British Empire, coloured red, and where the sun never set.

In junior high school I was subjected to a nun-centered geography education. Sister Connors utilized the chocolate-bar-maps every day and wielded a four-foot hardwood pointer on the map to help us locate various geographical features, and on our knuckles to help us pay attention. Sister Connors made us memorize stuff. She'd point to a country and expect to hear, without delay, its name, capital city, and chief exports. Sister Connors believed in respect, rote-retention, and the rule of law.

In addition to the chocolate-bar maps, all of our classrooms had other common elements. A Canadian flag was mandatory (the old one with the Union Jack in the corner), as was a picture of Queen Elizabeth, a photo of Pope John XXIII, a broken pencil sharpener, and a globe. The globe was a compliment to the chocolate-bar maps (we also had one at home in our living room; you don't see living room globes much these days). At school the globe was at the back of the classroom on a big table right beside a fifty pound "Funk and Wagnall's" dictionary. There was also a smelly geranium on that table, and a dangerously large paper cutter.

The paper cutter had a razor-sharp cutting arm at least two feet long, suitable for paper, sheet metal work, or amputating a child's hand if that became necessary. It had been donated to the school by Maximillian Robespierre. The French Revolution was over and he was done with it.

In grade nine Sister Aquinas used the globe and the maps to explain the mapping technique called *Mercator projection* that allowed curved surfaces to be represented on a flat surface. I was so intrigued by it that I briefly aspired to be a cartographer, an ambition quickly replaced by professional baseball.

Sister Aquinas is the nun that taught me the four-colour map theory which held that no more than four colours were necessary on any map to ensure that no two adjacent countries were the same colour, regardless of the shape of these areas. I was fascinated by this theorem and spent many hours trying to prove it wrong. No luck, so far.

These days I know we all can sit at the kitchen table with our laptop loaded with Google Maps, visit any country in the world, and extract data of staggering depth and unimaginable detail. Using *street-view* we can walk the avenues of any of the world's great cites. And we can ask Siri or Alexis or any other of our imaginary friends for a response to any inquiry we can dream of.

But here's the thing. When it comes to geography, it doesn't seem to be working. I say we bring back the chocolate-bar maps, the pointer and the globe. And the guillotine paper cutter, in case there are any discipline problems.

Assassination and Confession

Memories are hazy, imprecise things, stored in unreliable containers with dim and dusty corners.

Some experiences are beneath memory, some just below the surface, and some must be dredged from the murky bottom. An interesting aspect of remembering, especially unforeseen remembering, is the variety and power of the prompts that elicit memory in unexpected and inscrutable ways. The associations that trigger memory's nebulous retrievals are not always predictable, or lucid, or rational.

Recently, I've been reading about the controversy surrounding Bill 21 in Quebec, the secularism legislation that would prohibit authority figures—such as teachers, police officers, judges, prison guards—from wearing religious symbols (the Muslim hijab, Jewish kippah, or Sikh turban) while at work. Some of the complex polemics and principles surrounding this legislation (a serious and consequential debate left to better-qualified analysts) are recently articulated in numerous newspaper articles.

While I was lately reading one of these columns, it provoked one of those unpredictable (and somewhat irrational) retrievals from memory's dusty corners.

I was reminded of conversations and tribulations that occurred on a bright autumn afternoon about fifty-six years ago, events that included the rituals of Catholic schoolchildren going to confession, the death of an American president, the conventions of head-covering in church, a red-haired girl named Kathleen, and an eager boy named Pat McGinn. (The recollections recounted below may be appreciated only by those over sixty-five whose early instruction took place in a Catholic school among the sins and graces of a nun-centered education.)

In September 1963, Pat, Kathleen, and I were in grade nine, our last year with the nuns before the Reformation—exposure in grade ten to the Protestant population in a much larger regional high school. During grade nine, Sister Donovan was at the front of the room.

A couple of days before we started school in September, Martin Luther King Jr. delivered his "I Have a Dream" speech in Washington; in October, the Los Angeles Dodgers won the World Series (sweeping the Yankees in four games); and in November, John F. Kennedy was shot in Dallas.

In October, my friend Pat McGinn—a nascent social activist—started a petition (a partition, he called it) to close our school during the World Series.

As these events unfolded, we were subjected to a religious surge, a last-minute fortification before leaving the protective cover of the Holy Spirit and exposure to the evils of Protestantism. For Pat and me, 1963 was our last year of service as altar boys. We were honourably discharged. Anxiety related to eternal salvation gave way to concern for peer approval. And although altar-boying was abandoned in grade nine, the rituals of the confessional remained, for one final year, embedded in our schedules. Every other Friday (in preparation for the temptations of the weekend), we left school early and sashayed down to the Catholic church to purge, cleanse, and confess.

Our attitude toward confession had improved since the early grades, where the sacrament seemed ominous and fearful. There were anxious moments when the priest drew back the velvet curtain in dim light and obliged divulging secrets through the ornate screen to his unseen face in the shadows. And in preparation, we had to catalogue and quantify our sins. The importance of this inventory was seasonally adjusted. The nuns, always helpful, explained that before Christmas and Easter, more detail and accuracy were necessary. In early days, I thought if I omitted a sin, or fudged the numbers, God would stop my heart. I prayed that He would help me get the numbers right and provide direction for my life—the little time I had left.

But by grade nine, the stigma and shame attached to every small transgression was weakening. Sin was less threatening and had assumed a different status, which included a bonding effect among the boys, drawing us together in the great fraternity of sinners, brothers in iniquity.

One confessional Friday sticks with me.

It is generally agreed that most in my generation can remember the JFK assassination in Dallas and what they were doing when they first heard about it; maybe not everyone remembers that it happened on Friday.

That particular Friday—November 22, 1963—our class sat in a pew near the back of the cavernous Catholic church waiting our turn to enter the confessional (Pat called it the penalty box) one at a time. We all knew the drill. "Bless me, Father, for I have sinned; it has been two weeks since my last confession. . ." followed by a fairly standard "sinventory" that included sins of commission (things you did but shouldn't have done, like fighting, fibbing, and fecken around) and sins of omission (things you didn't do but should have done, like neglecting your chores, ignoring the indigent, and not feeling badly often enough).

The Ten Commandments provided (in convenient tablet form, Pat said) the underlying documentation for reckoning sins, but they were only a rough guide. As far as we knew, no one had manufactured graven images, killed anyone, coveted his neighbour's wife, or committed idolatry, against which the prophets railed.

When it came to properly enumerating sins in grade nine, the go-to sin (for boys at least) was impure thoughts (a.k.a. sins against purity). Impure thoughts were the staple of the male adolescent penitent. Here was a sin that had the dependability and predictability not found in the other sins. You didn't worry about quantifying impure thoughts. Nobody knew the number; it changed from minute to minute.

QUESTIONABLE COMMENTARY

McGinn, a recidivist impure thinker, told us he once claimed one thousand sins against purity and the priest snorted loud enough to be heard in the back pews. To simplify the enumeration, Pat speculated about applying our recently learned algebra skills: "Bless me, Father... since my last confession, I had impure thoughts x times... Solve for x." Pat also claimed impure thoughts caused pimples.

Males entering a Catholic church were required by statute to remove their hats. Females were required to put them on, or at least to display a head covering of some sort. Consequences for uncovered female heads included excommunication, fingernail splinters, and after-school detention. Forgetful grade nine girls going to confession were not exempted from the head-covering requirement. Hatless girls arriving at the steps of the church were required to innovate. The nuns decreed that any object placed on the head would meet the requirements. Standard solutions included handkerchiefs, Kleenex, and, occasionally, a single glove, the mate of which was either pocketed or lent to a hatless girlfriend. If girls hoped to enter the church without penalty, they understood that the demands of reverence trumped fashion—a head covering of some sort was commanded. Had an urn been available, it could be placed on the head, like the upright women of Judea heading for the village well.

Among fourteen-year-old boys, whispering and carrying on while awaiting entry to the penalty box, the head-covering issue required some discussion. If a Kleenex met the requirements, what about a Kleenex torn in half, or each piece torn in half again? Sister Donovan had taught us about exponential growth and decay. Could a piece of Kleenex reduced by half until it was barely visible to the naked eye save a girl from sin and admonition?

On the Days of Atonement, Kathleen (of the red hair) always remembered to bring her hat. She needed it to keep her brain warm, ready to meet any cerebral conundrums that might arise in the confessional. Kathleen was the top student in our school and the holiest girl in grade nine. Everyone agreed she was sinless. Kathleen was filled with scruples to the very top. We called her the Divinity.

High-minded conversations among the boys waiting to confess included (in addition to the head-covering seminar) speculation about what the Divinity might possibly divulge—did she forget to put the butter back in the fridge? Did she make a mistake doing long division? Or was she late returning a library book?

That Friday in November, we wittered, whispered, and waited our turn. We went to the box, completed the ritual, emerged and knelt to say our penance—three Hail Mary's were the mandatory minimum. Then, with the catharsis completed and guilt assuaged, we knew we could go outside and enjoy ourselves. Salvation agreed with us. We emerged from the dark church squinting in the November sunlight.

To our surprise and confusion, nuns, teachers, and various other adults were gathered on the church steps, crying, whispering, and commiserating. The news was passed around that John Fitzgerald Kennedy, the first Catholic president of the United States (and an Irishman, to boot) had been shot in Dallas. By a crackpot, someone supposed; he wasn't dead yet, they said, but all reports were that he soon would be.

Among the adults we knew, JFK had roughly the same status as Pope Paul VI, John the Baptist, and Bing Crosby. Later that evening, I recall CBS news anchor Walter Cronkite on TV taking off his glasses to wipe the tears from his eyes and announce that the president was dead. At suppertime, my mother was visibly distraught, but was still able to serve up the fishcakes and beans.

On Monday, Pat McGinn and I talked about the events of Friday.

He claimed that he saw the Divinity coming out of church with a glove on her head. McGinn was adamant; on the day Kennedy was shot, Kathleen forgot her hat. We should have known something bad was going to happen.

Nuns, Law and Order

About fifty years ago, when I was in high school, my malleable childhood ambitions included replacing Carl Yastrzemski playing left field for the Boston Red Sox; and if that didn't work out, I thought maybe I'd go to law school.

As it turned out, the lawyering aspiration wasn't realized either, but I was oddly reminded of it recently after my inexpert reading of the recent Supreme Court of Canada's decision that permitted Provincial Law Societies to deny accreditation to graduates of Trinity Western Law School. After some extemporaneous reflection on my early school experiences (in the context of the current post Charter, court activist, regulatory environment) I was left thinking that it's just as well I didn't bother with Law School because (today at least) my non-secular schooling may not meet the standard.

If I understand correctly, the Court determined that Law Societies have authority to deny accreditation because Trinity Western had excluded certain applicants by requiring them to sign a community covenant that obliged abstention from sexual activity except in the boundaries of a heterosexual marriage. Justices concluded that such exclusionary religious practices are not always protected by the Charter of Rights and that provincial administrative tribunals (Law Societies) were acting within their mandate; apparently, one exclusion rationalized the other. The court also decided that Law Societies have a legitimate obligation to uphold a positive public perception of the legal profession-- in itself, an ambitious undertaking.

Years ago, my experiences in a publically funded Catholic school may have involved exclusionary religious practices (sincerely held), as well as some discriminatory exclusions (both explicit or implicit) that probably restricted enrolment in a prejudicial manner, discouraged pluralism, and ensured my nun-centered learning did not include a lot of diversity. Sister Donovan made sure of that.

Every attitude and activity fell under the protective umbrella of the priests, prophets, and Pharisees in our local diocese. We were taught by nuns housed in a convent/rookery next to the school, we started school thirty minutes early so we could memorize the Baltimore Catechism, we ate fish on Friday, and every second Monday we walked down to the church to scrub the stains from our souls in the confessional box. Every student understood that the Pope's infallibility trickled down undiminished through the Church hierarchy until it reached the nun at the front of the classroom. In this environment there were no non-participants or conscientious objectors. Sister Donovan (at least nominally, a Sister of Charity) patrolled the hallways protecting us from interlopers (Protestants) and apostates. Heterodoxy and sacrilege needed to be guarded against. She walked those halls in a long black veil.

For the nuns, a community covenant was not needed to deter prohibited behaviour. They relied on guilt/shame coupled with ominous reminders of eternal damnation. Sister Donovan explained that (given our proclivity for sin) if we didn't feel guilty, then we should be ashamed of ourselves. Sister also clarified that Catholic boys were designed so they could burn without being consumed--a characteristic that allowed them (if necessary) to burn in hell forever. With these deterrents in place, signing community covenants seemed redundant.

If my experiences were repeated today—given the apparent limitations of the Charter to protect religious freedoms and the Supreme Court's deference to administrative panels—I can imagine that state-sponsored tribunals (or Spanish Inquisitors) might question my worthiness for the legal profession. My professional baseball career isn't working out either.

Soothing September

Long before bad grammar became a political asset and friending became a verb, my grade twelve Latin teacher taught me that September (the first of the ember months) was the seventh month (Latin: septem) in the old Roman calendar that had only ten months.

Not surprisingly, the seventh month was followed by the eighth (octo), the ninth (novem), and tenth (decem). These days, there are twelve months in the calendar year, subject to adjustment by an act of our provincial legislature, which is recently back in session.

Mrs. Senescent also explained that (a few years before she started teaching) Galileo Galilei tried to tell his Italian comrades that it was the sun—not the Earth—that was at the centre of our universe, and as a result, he was condemned as a heretic. Galileo's heliocentric view sounded like Protestantism to the Roman pope who thought all of God's heavenly bodies must revolve around him. (Galileo had no way of knowing that one day we would discover that the universe actually revolves around Donald Trump—a doctrine currently held by cable news networks, and soon enacted into law, if things go according to plan.)

Fortunately for us, Galileo and Mrs. Senescent were right about the sun-centered world. Apparently this detail, along with the tilt of the Earth's axis (and other factors I've forgotten) result in the changing seasons and our (often understated) enjoyment of these transitions. Among the seasons available to Nova Scotians, it seems to be generally agreed upon—at least among folks my age—that autumn is the most favoured.

And September and October in particular are such well-mannered and generous months that we are willing to set aside the dismal reality that winter is just around the corner—and God knows how that will turn out.

In this province, everybody understands that the fall weather is lovely—no sense going on about it. Not to mention the leaves and the colours, the sun lights the water at an improved angle, mornings are crisper, nights are cooler, and bugs are scarce. Adjectives like *blustery, bright, cool, earthy,* and *vibrant* get used more frequently. Farmers' markets, fall fairs, and church suppers re-emerge, sweaters are taken from the backs of closets, school buses reappear, and first-day-of-school photographs are posted on Facebook. The kids all have big smiles and backpacks. These pictures provoke optimism and promise.

And in September, people become more sensible. This is because September restores some structure to the anarchy of the summer. It sends kids back to school, resets reasonable bedtimes, renders meal-times predictable, closes cottages, and pulls boats from the lake.

Shorter days and improved humidity mean a better sleep. And while enjoying the comfortable evening air, recovering vacationers mutate into functional, rational adults. People will make predictable jokes about getting back to work to get some rest (they all had a wonderful holiday, but are so glad to be home). They will talk about high blood pressure and the wonders of foreign travel. Later in the month, following the autumn equinox, additional sanity will be restored. Days of leisure are transformed into calendared events with organization and routine. Random abstract becomes concrete sequential.

Of course, for younger people, the pivotal event is return to school, with all of its excitements, anticipations, and anxieties. Dormant perceptions are awakened—the sound of the school bus coming down the road, the foul smell of the diesel, the feel of new clothes, new experiences, new relationships, the comfort of new running shoes, the smell of new textbooks, possibly some new learning.

And in spite of contrary claims, students are glad to get back, looking forward to seeing friends again, busy asking all the essential questions—*who's your teacher? Who's in your class? Did you get a top locker? Can I put your number in my phone? Did you see what Olivia was wearing?*

Later, at suppertime, parents everywhere will ask, "What did you do in school today?" Among students, the answer is universally agreed upon: "Nothing." They have all signed non-disclosure agreements.

Kids have it tough these days, relentlessly inundated with media that notify them how to act, what to wear, and what constitutes acceptance. They have no relief from the television where the adults never act like adults, and where reality shows have nothing to do with reality.

When not distracted by a screen that allows censure and intimidation twenty-four hours a day, they face a demanding curriculum that includes ominous and unavoidable math classes. Students are understandably muddled by conflicting messages and nuanced contradictions, confused by emerging sexuality and identity. In their lunch bag, they may have an apple that self-identifies as an orange.

Children come to school from every possible social and economic circumstance. Some are affluent, some are poor, and some are impoverished. They come healthy, ill, damaged, intact, confident, anxious, eager, and passive. Some are curious, some distracted, some arrive bubbling with enthusiasm, and some are dulled with indifference. Many are gifted with large ideas and some are not. Some are hungry. All have an equal right to opportunity, and good teachers are acutely aware that they have an obligation to provide it.

In September, this onerous obligation causes, among teachers, an apprehension and nervousness of their own. Teachers sense the obligation and they are not unaffected by it. They may understand the prescribed curriculum, but they also know the most durable of the lessons they will deliver are ones of compassion and kindness. September can be hard on students and teachers. We should treat them both with care.

But for retired guys like me, we don't have to go back to work (this is the central concept of retirement), and we are delighted that October baseball gets interesting in the post-season, that hockey will be back on television, and that soon we can reintroduce oatmeal for breakfast.

We start to think about painting the trim around the back door, putting away the BBQ, taking the chairs off the deck. There's no hurry. We're happy we don't have to mow the lawn so often and that the days are getting shorter—this means we don't have to wait so long to go to bed. All is well. Nova Scotians are probably right about the fall.

Enough about that; as my Uncle Joseph used to say, the shadows are lengthening and cocktail hour beckons. Uncle Joe was quite old, but when he found himself sitting in front of a glass of beer, he was never confused about what to do with it.

QUESTIONABLE COMMENTARY

Sticking Up for the Irish

I had a good chat with my friend and fellow pensioner Albert the other day while we were waiting to have our vehicles serviced at the Ford dealership – nice people there in the service department, and free coffee. We had about an hour's wait, and time to kill.

Albert was in fine form and, as always, generous with unsolicited advice and unfiltered opinion. Whenever we get together we tend to review recent news articles, and generally improve the coverage in ways that may be invisible to others. For Albert, it only takes one article to get him going, and then he branches out.

Last week an opinion piece suggested that the manner in which the English have historically treated the Irish people is analogous to the indifference that self-absorbed Americans display toward Canadians. Albert didn't see it quite the same way. He claims his ancestors were taken barefoot from the peat bogs of Donegal and forced by famine across the Atlantic. "And their socio-economic status," he said, "the same as described by all Irish mothers; they didn't have a pot to piss in." This rich heritage, Albert says, entitles him to a point of view.

"It may be a bit of a stretch," he said, "for Mr. Leger to imagine that the indignities or indifference we Canadians have suffered, at the hands of the Americans, are analogous to the Irish experience. Canada, as far as I know, did not endure the Viking, Norman, or Cromwellian invasions, or Henry VIII, or the dissolution of the monasteries, or the penal laws, or the horror of absentee landlords exporting food during a national famine. To say nothing", he continued, "of the lovely Queen Elizabeth I, who was anxious to suppress Irish culture, especially the music provided by Irish harpists whom she hoped to discourage by removing their fingernails or hanging them. Harpers hanged by the English; the Irish say they died suddenly. And in case that didn't work, the Virgin Queen made arrangements to burn their hand-crafted harps.

"So yeah," Albert said, "maybe Leger's analogy is a little weak. Sure, the current president may be a self-serving, narcissistic megalomaniac, but if he has plans to buy the CBC or send Jared Kushner north to burn all the hockey sticks, I'm not aware of it." (Here, Albert paused to point out that during the last federal election, he had––like Queen Elizabeth––displayed some anti-Harper sentiment.)

"But," Albert conceded, "I may have to renovate my opinion; it's easy to imagine that emerging nationalism, immigration anxiety, and the current Brexit divorce proceedings have rekindled some Irish/English hostility." "But," he said, "I'd like to think the residue from this unfortunate colonial history is water mostly under the bridge, and I'm a bit puzzled by the animosity––even hatred–– claimed by Mr. Leger. And any suggestion that England, rightly or wrongly, does not have a legitimate democratic option to leave the EU, or that the England people are utterly unconcerned about a hard border between Northern Ireland and the Republic, I just can't accept it.

"The Brexit situation reminds me of a novel I read forty years ago," Albert said, "*Puckoon*, written by the great philosopher Spike Milligan, whose Irish father got along just fine with his English mother. The protagonist, a character called Dan Milligan, is leading a life of carefree indifference in a small Irish village (Puckoon), when he is caught up in an argument about where (following the 1921 partition) the border separating Northern Ireland from the Irish Republic should be located. Dan and his pals, and the Boundary Commission, are anxious to get the matter sorted out in just one evening––before the pub closes. As a result, the border is drawn carelessly and arbitrarily through the middle of their town and, as it turns out, through the middle of the pub. Without prudence or forethought, the boundary decision reached by the Guinness drinkers is immediately approved, and army checkpoints are set up overnight. The citizens of Puckoon wake up the next morning to find they cannot move freely from one side of the street to the other. Churches are separated from graveyards (the newly deceased need a passport to be buried), and houses are estranged from their outhouses. Worst of all, pub-patrons had to squeeze into one corner because the beer is cheaper in the British territory.

"The lads didn't take the time to think it through," Albert said. "I'm not sure if Theresa May has read *Puckoon*, but if not, I'm willing to lend her a copy."

Albert has a number of sentiments to be shared, digested, and confronted. I have asked him on different occasions why he doesn't record some of his opinions, write some of this stuff down, maybe author a book. "Yeah," he said, "I've thought about it, but I just can't be bothered. I have the time, but not the inclination.

"You know, years ago, my Uncle Pat wrote a book––more of a personal memoir––nobody would publish it, but he did have a single copy printed. It ended up in the attic of his house where the mice chewed off one corner off it." Borrowing from Bernard Shaw, Albert added, "Even the mice couldn't finish it."

"And," he said, "in my case, I'm not sure if I have the patience. In fact, for those of us living off our pensions and our wits––both deficient––I'm not sure anymore if patience is a virtue at all. We don't have time to be patient.

"I'm like the 'Albert Clock'," he said. And immediately he began to clarify his comment with another yarn. "In the eastern end of the great city of Belfast, where the Titanic was launched in 1911 (the Irish say it was fine when it left), stands the Albert Memorial Clock Tower. It was built on the marshy ground reclaimed from the Farset River, and as a result, the clock tower is tilted four feet off perpendicular. This slant prevents the clock mechanism from keeping time properly. Grinning, the local Irish say that Old Albert may not have the time, but he has the inclination.

"Sort of like me," Albert said. "Although, thank God, I've never been married to Queen Victoria. She has a face like a boiled ham."

"In any case, I can't support Mr. Leger's contention that we are to Americans what the Irish are to the English. This equivalence seems a bit pessimistic, a bit gloomy––as gloomy as Paddy Cleary who sold burial plots in Donegal, door to door. Paddy's argument was that burial is healthier than cremation. And either one is better than spending the evening with Theresa May."

Albert was anxious to ventilate his opinions on a number of other subjects, but the service guy came over and told him his car was ready.

Trump and My Mother

A recent newspaper article reports that while President Trump was speaking to a group of business owners in Washington, he accused Canadians of smuggling goods into Canada in order to avoid "massive tariffs." As an example of our egregious behaviour, Trump suggested that clandestine Canadians regularly slip across the border, buy themselves a pair of shoes, scuff them up to make them look worn, and smuggle them home.

For me, the President's comments precipitated an involuntary flashback from about sixty years ago. I think Trump was talking about my mother.

In the 1950s and 60s I attended elementary school in Fredericton, and every summer, as the school year was approaching, our family headed for Calais Maine (just across the bridge in St. Stephen) for school supplies. I'm not sure if our contact with the world's most powerful nation was the result of massive tariffs, the nuances of international currency exchange, or scarce monetary supply within our family, but my father insisted we could save money if we took a trip *across the line* to purchase school supplies, school clothes, and new shoes. At the time, my mother (for whom foot care had a high profile) insisted that we wear Savage shoes. Savage shoes were, apparently, the best available for growing children, and even if they were two sizes too big we would grow into them.

On the way back home, before we got to the border checkpoint, we always stopped at the side of the road, tore tags and labels off new clothes, stuffed them up under the dash (the border patrol would never think to look there), and buried stuff among old clothes in our cardboard suitcases. Most remarkably, exactly as Mr. Trump indicated this week, my mother told us to scuff up our new Savage shoes in the roadside gravel, put them on our feet, and keep our mouths shut.

At the Customs my father did all the talking, and we were soon on our way home and drove the rest of the way gratefully, as if we had escaped detection crossing into West Berlin. The trips to Maine were part of my early education in economics and morality. I learned that some crimes, such as international trafficking in children's clothing, are not only forgivable but praiseworthy. I remember my surprise that my pious, ultra-nervous, risk-averse mother was surprisingly calm, as if she was quite used to the excitement of living life on the fringes of the law. In fact, she was silently saying the rosary. She always had her rosary available for just such an emergency.

I don't know what President Eisenhower was thinking, but all of this could have been easily avoided if he'd just built a wall on New Brunswick's western border.

FOGGY RECOLLECTIONS

Writing Stuff Down

Our local newspaper has reported that Nova Scotia's population increased last year at a rate almost equal to the national average, and that last year we added more than 10,000 residents.

Apparently, we now have more Nova Scotians over sixty-five than we have children under fifteen, and the ratio of seniors to children will continue to increase until, in about ten years, a quarter of Nova Scotians will be over sixty-five, eligible for seniors' discounts and preferred parking.

Recently, for the first time, millennials in the workforce outnumber baby boomers, and (another sobering reality) in the coming decades, our retirement-age population may become larger than the working-age population.

Among those concerned about health care, pension plans, solvency, incontinence, and replacement parts, this data is disconcerting.

Some of the oldest cohort of baby boomers (the early boomers, conceived in the exuberance following the Second World War) have recently migrated into their seventies, and most of these are retired, or at least beginning to step back, to leave the stage.

Some will leave the farm…

And because boomers are allegedly responsible for the current state of the Western world, plenty has been written about the range of attributes associated with their generation—their virtues and extravagances, and the environmental excesses. Not to mention, the isolation, loneliness, untapped expertise, financial uncertainties, stubbornness, flawed memory, driving habits, and generalized wear and tear.

I'm told that boomers control much of the country's discretionary spending, and market researchers have *mined the data* related to boomers' buying habits, travel practices, leisure activities, and happy-hour preferences. Trends indicate that it may be time to buy a few shares in companies that produce comfortable slippers, anti-wrinkle creams, or incontinence trousers (*no need to wrap them, dear; I'll wear them home*).

QUESTIONABLE COMMENTARY

Say what you want about old dogs...

For me, at least, it's not clear why market researchers are interested in the early boomers. Among my limited social network, the general sentiment is that (apart from groceries, paper towels, and batteries for the remote), we have mostly everything we need, and we won't be buying much at all when it comes to day-to-day consumer products.

Insofar as I am able to judge (not far), many of us may never have to buy another pair of dress shoes, or a tie, or a hairbrush. And we have shirts and underwear we've been trying to wear out for years—you wash the car with them, clean the oven, throw them in the washer, and they're as good as new.

But more interesting than the consumer habits of early boomers, demographers have identified a few behavioural changes, thereby demonstrating that at least some of us are capable of adjustment, no matter what people say about old dogs and new tricks. Among these late-onset behavioural renovations, there are a couple that are of particular interest: the recent disciples and the amateur memoirists.

Recent disciples: Many of the boomer congregation have become more attentive to actuarial statistics, expectancy tables, and the mathematics of mortality. We note with interest the ages of those in the obit column, we check out our ancestral longevity, and we find ourselves doing the math on certain long-term investments and purchases (*Do I really need those thirty-year shingles?*). Some folks discuss these calculations under the heading "cemetery arithmetic."

And apparently, a significant number of boomers—lately more aware of the ephemeral nature of life—have started going back to church, or at least have become more spiritual, more involved in religious activity.

Maybe these prodigal seniors are returning at the eleventh hour because they are more alert to the fragility and brevity of life. Or maybe on Sunday morning they have time to kill before lunch. A friend of mine refers to this rediscovered spirituality among the elderly as "cramming for the final."

Valediction becomes benediction...

Of course, serious people may consider a return to the faith of their fathers for all the right reasons. Some of those for whom belief is gone consider it an escape from orthodoxy and remain proudly defiant. Others, who passed hectic lives preoccupied with worldly concerns, are confused in their retirement years by unexpected moments of loneliness, or a sense of vacancy in their lives.

Thoughts may drift toward mortality (a concept previously not included in their consciousness, even though they knew their ancestors were afflicted by it), and seniors discover that when facing the realities of illness, declining productivity, and the death of friends, rationality has its limitations.

Because funerals are often religious events, late returnees to the flock can rest assured (and in peace) that any spiritual recovery will be mentioned in their end-of-life valediction. At funerals, the virtues conferred by death are miraculously retroactive. For some attendees, the eulogy may include new information, received with a sense of discovery. Valediction becomes benediction.

... The deceased toward the end was restored to grace. After dieting, downsizing, and decluttering, he made an effort to simplify his life. His residential and corporal downsizing was followed by other spiritual expansions and material contractions. During the last two years, the deceased was a regular at church suppers that involved baked beans, or salt cod and fish cakes. And he attended bingo every month, and even appeared at church from time to time, sometimes staying for the entire service ...

And even if late-onset spiritual remediation doesn't include formal religion, many seniors will tend toward a more reflective, introspective demeanour—a contemplation of their days. This type of thoughtful examination is generally beneficial, but it may also have elements of risk and recklessness.

While he was on trial in ancient Greece for corrupting youth, Socrates professed that the unexamined life is not worth living, and he was sentenced to death. A couple of thousand years later, the great American satirist Kurt Vonnegut reminded us of the perils of the examined life: "What about if you examine it closely and it turns out to be a clunker?"

Notwithstanding, proclivity toward nostalgic reminiscence often includes an impulse to leave behind a record, some documentation of a life. This inclination has spawned a species of late-onset chroniclers.

In any case, we know that people who have drifted into age become reminiscent, and although many of their indulgences are sadly gone, they happily remember how glorious they once were. They want to talk about old times.

Deep thinkers claim there is a compelling psychological need for older adults to leave behind selected portions of their story.

While technology provides the means, the conditions that motivate seniors to document their experiences are not always clear (self-aggrandizement, apology, revenge, etc.), but usually it involves some understanding that compelling one's recollections, organizing one's thoughts, or simply writing stuff on the computer screen may help aging authors to make sense of their lives.

Some wish to pass along accumulated insights or influence how they are remembered. Others realize that their children provide the only immortality available to them.

Whatever the motivation, the resulting recollections will inevitably be a bit distorted. They will include a little fabrication and conjecture (with age, things can be reimagined and rearranged), and besides, the clinically accurate version of events can be hazardous. Astute memoirists will appreciate that the experiences they document may be interesting in ways that are invisible to others.

So it is that some thoughtful folks recommend against amateur memoirs, especially those recalling experiences that were tiresome and ordinary at the time, but that are now imagined as fascinating.

Some suggest that those who feel compelled to record portions of an earlier life be reminded that two advantages are gained if the writing is put off as long as possible: The first benefit is that the project may be forgotten and abandoned altogether, and the second advantage is that the risks involved with pruning or polishing will be reduced because many contemporaries will be safely dead, and thus less likely to challenge the account.

I'm not one of those. My advice is to go full-steam ahead and write some stuff down—everything you can think of. It'll do you good, even if nobody reads it. It will trigger forgotten indulgences, and elicit recollections of old friends you haven't thought about in years, possibly obliging you to get in touch with some of them to clarify a common experience, verify a half-remembered lie, or review a questionable assumption. In all cases, the benefits of restoring old friendships are always greater than we calculate.

So those wafting into senility may spend some of their time rummaging through the lost-and-found box looking for understanding—or contemplating the incomprehensible, or briefly considering the obtuse mysteries of existence.

Or, as suppertime approaches, they may ask themselves weighty questions like, *Why daylight saving time?* Or *Can I love Kraft Dinner and still be a good person?*

The handicaps of aging sometimes include digression and incoherence. There's evidence of it everywhere.

WILLIAM J. KILFOIL

The Sixth Toe

My grandmother had six toes on one foot. At least that was the belief shared by us, her grandchildren, when we were kids.

It wasn't Grandma herself who claimed an extra toe (she never mentioned body parts of any kind), but everyone else talked about it and the account of the extra digit became part of our childhood experience. No one could ever explain how the rumour got started, but the story gained momentum because it could not be disproved.

No one ever saw Grandma's bare feet (*No eyes save those of God beheld them*), but for several years, even in the absence of eyewitness testimony, the presence of the surplus toe was accepted as fact, much like Santa Claus.

Especially among the grandchildren, the six-toe narrative was propagated and celebrated. We wanted it to be true. Eleven toes set our grandmother apart from the other garden-variety grandmothers. It improved our social status when explaining the surplus to our schoolmates. If our proclamation was not met with the expected shock and awe, we added drama by claiming that it was an extra big toe—*yeah, really... another big toe ... it's right there beside the other one ...*

During the years that I remember my grandmother, she always looked the same. She exuded a sense of tranquil dignity while she stood at the kitchen table making bread and sugar cookies, her domestic orbit always within a five-foot radius of the kitchen stove.

She was soft and fleshy and wore a big apron over a long patterned dress. Her apple doll face was topped by a swarm of grey hair held up by oversized hairpins the size of coat hangers.

And on her feet, the same black leather shoes and heavy surgical stockings around her swollen ankles (to stem the progression of her phlebitis). And always the apron. Only her asbestos arms and bread-dough face were visible to us. We knew Grandma had asbestos hands and arms because she could reposition hardwood burning deep in the firebox of her cooking stove without injury or concern.

In the evenings, she'd sit and talk, and put a burned-out light-bulb inside the heel of a wool sock so it would keep its shape while she mended it. It was a matter of survival. Bread needed to be made, feet needed to be kept warm. The weather needed to be talked about.

In living memory, no one had ever set foot in Grandma's small bedroom by the kitchen. Children in particular were forbidden under penalty of death. It was *Grammy's room*. She had suffered there. When we reached the age of reason, she sat each of us down on a kitchen chair and issued a *fatwa* defining the exclusion zone—not to be ignored if we wanted to live a long and happy life. During the period of this prohibition, we assumed Grandma would go to her grave with those terrible compression stockings on, leaving the digital redundancy mystery unresolved.

But when I was about twelve years old, an unexpected breakthrough befell, and the extra-toe investigation was reopened.

One evening during the Christmas holiday, my sister and I discovered Grandma sitting in a kitchen chair by the woodstove, soaking her feet in a galvanized tin washtub filled with steaming hot water, yellowed by Dettol. The temptation that presented itself could only be yielded to. With fear and trepidation, we approached the washtub and furtively scanned the pale, wrinkled feet in the yellow water. We got a pretty good look at them before she told us to buzz off.

It turned out there was some truth to it.

There was definitely a discernible branch off the little toe folded into the one beside it. It was not much more than a pea-sized lump, but you could see how that rumour got started. My sister and I bolted from the kitchen, disillusioned. We were anticipating something far more conspicuous, more sensational.

To make things worse, the night before this exculpatory foot-soaking episode, we had overheard cousins sharing new and disheartening information related to Santa Claus. We went to bed low-spirited.

So it was that during that memorable Christmas season, Santa Claus and the six-toe hypothesis were laid to rest. Life can be harsh. The world teaches you things.

Soaking feet has, in recent generations, fallen from fashion. In old days, foot problems had more prominence, more cachet. Old people could spend a whole evening talking about corn plasters, bunions, fungus, fallen arches, and plantar fasciitis. They soaked their feet in hot water poured from the tea kettle, with pant legs rolled up, both feet in a worn metal basin (enamel-ware) with a splattered-paint finish and black patches on the rim. The water had to be as hot as any human could bear—half a degree below the boiling point was ideal—and saturated with Epsom salt, vinegar, baking soda, Dettol, apple cider, or horse liniment.

Epsom salt in particular was effective. In addition to sore feet, Epsom salts cured cataracts and straightened bowed legs and crooked teeth. It also resolved issues related to personal beauty and gardening. My father had a relationship with Epsom salt. Some days, he'd come home from work, sit down in the kitchen, take his shoes off and rub his feet. *My dogs are barking,* he'd say. His big Irish feet only fit in the basin one at a time, and the towel under it didn't keep water from splashing over the faded linoleum that covered the kitchen floor.

My father was a frugal man who kept his feet on the ground and the sky above. Only with the greatest effort was he able to set aside his natural parsimony and buy good-quality leather shoes which, resulting from his care and attention, lasted between twenty and thirty years.

To ensure this longevity, father owned a variety of shoe-related paraphernalia. He maintained a complete shoe-repair capability in our cellar, including awls, waxed thread, shoe stretchers, tack hammers, and the specialty pliers required by serious cobblers. The centrepiece of the shoe-repair theatre was a heavy cast-iron shoe anvil over which he could fit shoes upside-down to replace soles and heels.

In high school, I used the anvil and the tack hammer to add little crescent-shaped metal clickers to the heels of my shoes so that they would make tap-dancing noises when I walked on the asbestos tiles at school. In this way, I improved my social standing. Father also had a drawer of replacement rubber heels which, in the winter months, I whittled into a circular shape and used for hockey pucks.

My father of Irish ancestry has been dead for many years. His gravestone is etched with shamrocks and a Celtic cross. When we were young, he told us questionable stories about children getting through the winter months by carrying baked potatoes in cold hands and putting pepper in winter boots to warm their feet. Some of his stories were nearly true.

He once told us about a grave site at Glasnevin cemetery in Dublin with the inscription: *I told you my feet were killing me.*

My religious mother sometimes confused soaking feet with washing feet, which (she would remind us) is not just a matter of hygiene, but a ceremony rooted in Christian traditions. The Thursday before Easter (Maundy Thursday) commemorates the Washing of the Feet at the Last Supper when Jesus, in an effort to teach the virtue of humility, washed the feet of his disciples. And the

Bible tells us the story of Mary of Bethany who washed and anointed Jesus's feet in gratitude for raising her brother Lazarus from the dead, and in preparation for his burial.

I hope I am remembering those Bible stories properly. If not, I will happily—as a fellow with new orthopedic shoes on—stand corrected.

Smoking in the Glory Days

During the 1960s, when I was in high school, I (along with all my buddies) smoked cigarettes. Fortunately, during this period, instead of causing cancer, cigarettes stunted your growth. *You better give up those smokes*, we were told, *or they'll stunt your growth*. Cancer was never mentioned, just height. The growth-stunting hazard wasn't much of a deterrent.

More recently, as a result of current news articles, a couple of my fellow retirees and I have had clumsy conversations about the evils and injuries of vaping, and its odious comparisons to the cigarette-smoking generation we grew up in. Our discussion resolved nothing, but the prattle did provoke some distant and foggy memories of a couple of recidivist smokers, each of whom would easily qualify for the *Reader's Digest* designation of "My Most Unforgettable Character"—if anyone is old enough to remember that feature in the monthly edition.

One of these nicotine-addled eccentrics was my pipe-smoking grandfather (dead for forty years), and the other a former teacher colleague of mine, who is, surprisingly, still extant.

I'll get back to these scoundrels in a minute.

Apparently, there are people even smarter than psychologists who tell us that smells are among our strongest memory triggers. It seems to be about biology. They say the olfactory sense is directly connected to areas of the brain that are concerned with emotion and memory, especially childhood memories. Old folks in particular tend to experience this phenomenon—endless possibilities for unexpected recollections, provoked by a smell.

Fresh-baked biscuits, boiled cabbage on a wood stove, yeast and molasses, damp stone cellars, ploughed ground after a rain, wet woolen mittens on the furnace grate, the pee on a baby's leather shoes, a newly opened tin of tobacco.

And what about the smell of your Aunt Teresa's geraniums, the varnish and piety of the parish church, and the unimprovable barn smell of cow shit and straw?

And among these smells, the pleasant aroma of my grandfather's pipe tobacco was probably the most agreeable—that is, right up until he abandoned his pipe for the pleasures of roll-your-own cigarettes and chewing tobacco.

You don't come across many pipe smokers these days. Nearly extinct they are, although I can report a recent sighting on a September Saturday at a rural Petro-Can where I stopped for gas. An elderly white-haired man upholstered in tweed was at the counter paying his bill (with cash), puffing away on a crooked pipe, a white cloud around his head. No one complained about him smoking inside the building, and if they had, I am certain he wouldn't have paid the slightest attention. The old guy had leathery skin and one tooth (in the bottom). The sweet smell of the tobacco cloud that surrounded him was wonderful. After painstakingly counting his change, the pipe smoker issued a polite thank-you and left.

Setting aside for a minute the nefarious health issues, it's a shame about the scarcity of pipe smokers these days. I miss them.

Before the First World War, pipes, cigars, and chewing tobacco were the popular forms of tobacco consumption. In the muddy trenches of France, pipes and cigars were cumbersome and unmanageable, and tobacco companies sensed an opportunity. They sent millions of free cigarettes to the troops, donated money to the war effort, and generated advertisements that linked cigarette smoking to courage and patriotism.

The Great War spawned a generation of cigarette smokers, especially among women. Drinking and smoking were seen as evidence of liberation, worldliness, and sophistication. Women had earned the right to vote, work outside the home, and smoke to their hearts' content. And after the war, the focus of cigarette advertising shifted from patriotism to personal heath. Tobacco promotions included encouragement from family doctors claiming cigarettes were an aid to digestion; others featured children urging their mothers to start smoking as a calming therapy. Everyone smoked, including cowboys and camels.

My pipe-smoking maternal grandfather (Jack) was born in August of 1895 on the same day American outlaw John Wesley Hardin was shot dead in a saloon in Texas. He (Jack, not John Wesley) lived with my family for a period of time during the 1960s while I was in high school. My parents were part of the generation that was unequivocal about whose obligation it was to provide for parents in their old age. With a view to avoid freezing to death, Jack stayed with us during the winter months when the toilet water in his uninsulated bathroom froze over.

Throughout his life, Jack was a reliable and steadfast consumer of tobacco products. He also had a protracted, enthusiastic, and unhealthy relationship with alcohol.

In the early years of his annual winter layover at our house, Jack often sat on our back step chewing tobacco, spitting on the ground, and killing the grass within a four-foot radius.

Brown juice leaked from the corner of his mouth and stained his ultra-absorbent flannel shirt. My mother couldn't put up with the spitting and staining and issued a *fatwa* outlining a spitting/tobacco-chewing prohibition. As a compromise, she reluctantly agreed to allow her father to smoke cigarettes in our house. My mother ran a very tight ship. The smoking-in-the-house concession amazed us all.

Every day of his life, Jack wore a faded red flannel shirt, heavy wool pants, and industrial-strength long woolen underwear (the same ones) year-round (the one-piece variety with the trapdoor in the back). But for my mother's direct orders on wash day, these beauties would never have been separated from his body.

Jack was so thin (my mother said there was more meat on a hockey stick) that his woolen pants had to be held up with wide suspenders because a belt was useless on his hipless frame. One pocket of his flannel shirt was stuffed with cigarette papers, sulfur-smelling wooden matches (Eddy), and a distressed black rosary. The other pocket contained approximately fifty-one dog-eared bicycle playing cards and a bushel of lint. The deck of cards was kept at the ready in the event that any card-playing opportunity presented itself. The Eddy matches Jack found useful for picking his teeth, removing ear wax (and other debris), and igniting his hand-rolled cigarettes.

Jack's fingers were yellowed by the roll-your-own that was constantly in his hand or stuck to his lower lip. Although he had rolled thousands of cigarettes, he was remarkably unskilled at it, clumsiness no doubt the result of arthritic fingers and failing eyesight. Loose MacDonald's tobacco in a tin, together with his Zig-Zag papers, he referred to as *makins*. *Get me my makins*, he'd order me.

About every fifteen minutes, with tobacco all over his shirt and his lap, Jack fumbled with the papers and set about to manufacture a lumpy, ill-formed cigarette. When he brought his handiwork to his mouth, tobacco would often fall out of the end, so that when he ignited the wooden match (sometimes with a crusty, yellowed thumbnail, sometimes on the sole of his shoe), he didn't so much light his cigarette as set it on fire.

Jack hardly talked at all, just smoked and said the rosary, mumbling and grunting. He spit loose shreds of tobacco, and when the cigarette paper stuck to his lip, he was unbothered by the ashes that fell on his heavy flannel shirt. Just before it charred his flesh, Jack removed the cigarette butt from his mouth and crushed it out between his thumb and index finger.

A small amount of the debris from this activity would land in the heavy, brown glass ashtray (same colour as a beer bottle) that my mother had placed on the end table next to his chair.

With perceptions dulled by alcohol abuse, Grampa Jack was aloof and unobtrusive. Years of chronic pain caused by arthritis, encroaching senility, and chronic loneliness made him ill-tempered. It wasn't clear what memories gave him comfort or which regrets tormented him. His thin, arthritic fingers and hands were swollen and misshapen, and he had large ganglion cysts on his wrists. He wore heavy eyeglasses, which reminded me of the massive convex lens I'd seen at a maritime lighthouse. Jack had a permanent lump on his forehead, which was in danger of breaking through thin, waxy skin. His thick glasses alarmed me because of the way they magnified his milky, glaucoma eyes.

Sometimes after school, based on my mother's robust encouragement, my sister and I would "volunteer" to play cards with him. *It wouldn't kill you to play a few hands with your grandfather,* Mom would say; *supper will be ready in two shakes of a lamb's tail.* Jack played only one game—Auction-45s. He liked to win, and to improve his chances, he cheated.

Jack managed to have the ace of hearts every time he dealt the cards. It was never clear how he accomplished this sleight of hand, but apparently, his shaky, arthritic fingers could deal from the bottom of the deck. When I told my mother about the cheating, she laughed and said not to worry about it, just consider it part of the entertainment. While he was dealing, I carefully scrutinized my grandfather's knobby, onion-skinned hands, but I could never detect any misconduct.

QUESTIONABLE COMMENTARY

My mother accepted the burdens that were hers to bear. It was hard for her, watching her father on the edge of death—the flannel, the wool, the black beads, the ratty slippers. *Soon, he would go the way of all flesh.* This was the way she put it. Sitting in his chair, sometimes Jack scratched his nether parts. My mother's reaction to this behaviour was unfavourable.

She was always trying to get him up out of the chair to go for a bit of a walk. *You should get out and get the stink blown off you,* she'd say, adding, *and people die faster staying in one place.* My mother understood the irony of life's circle. Parents become children to their own.

My mother's remarkable wintertime concession that allowed her father to smoke in our house may have had something to do with the -10 degree temperatures on our back step, but more likely, it was about my mother's limitless capacity for compassion. Jack's wife (my grandmother) had died years earlier and, in the manner of many of the fathers of his generation, he was never really close to his children. He couldn't read due to failing eyesight, he spoke very little, and he didn't eat much of anything except oatmeal porridge (*stir-about,* he called it).

I didn't pay as much attention to my grandfather as I should have. Once, I watched him cheating while he was playing solitaire. Even back then, it struck me as troubling and incomprehensible. Cheating yourself seemed confusing. Instead of calling the game solitaire, Jack called it solitary, which, for him, it certainly was.

Occasionally, Jack would signal to us to come over to his chair. Without a word, he'd give us a coin (usually a quarter) he had hidden in the palm of his hand. Then he'd go back to smoking, scratching, saying the rosary.

Jump ahead fifteen years, long after Jack died.

It was the 1970s. I was teaching high school at a time when school secretaries smoked at their desks, principals smoked in their offices, teachers smoked in the staff rooms, and some high schools provided designated smoking rooms for students.

Among teachers I have known, none smoked with more enjoyment (or with more theatre) than a robust colleague of mine named Timothy.

At the time, staff members often played cards in the staff room over their lunch hour. Tim's lunchtime routine was as follows: Every day, he went to the school cafeteria and ordered an extra-large (cardboard) plate of French fries and gravy—nothing else, just fries with extra gravy. He came back to the staff room, sat down (breathing heavily) at the card table, and with anxious anticipation, placed the plate in front of him. Planted upright in the middle of the mound of fries, a plastic fork proclaimed territorial sovereignty while Tim paused to light a cigarette.

Before tucking into the grease, Tim inhaled deeply, brightening the end of his cigarette and creating a good inch of ash, which fell on the plate with the gravy. The most diverting aspect of the spectacle was that Tim started eating before exhaling, urgently shoveling in brown, gravy-dipped fries as white smoke leaked slowly from his nose and ears.

Tim stopped stoking in French fries only long enough to take another long haul off his cigarette—more ash in the gravy, and more smoke seeping and smoldering from every orifice. The fries, the gravy, and the cigarette were gone at the same time.

Tim finished his meal with a sigh and a sense of accomplishment, like a job well done. He'd wipe his mouth with the nearest piece of paper (the staff meeting agenda), belch loudly, and order whomever was holding the cards to deal him in. Tim repeated this ritual frequently during the two years I worked with him—right up until he went off on sick leave.

Two generations apart, chain smokers Jack and Tim were Unforgettable Characters for reasons I have not adequately explained here, their lives replete with comedy and tragedy. The world is full of a number of things.

Quantifying Happiness

A couple of recent columns in our local newspaper provoked some of the syrupy nostalgia recounted a few paragraphs below.

Apparently, a group called *Engage Nova Scotia* is determined to measure the quality of our lives (an ambitious undertaking) through a survey of eighty thousand Nova Scotians who will be asked questions across eight key areas: education, health, community vitality, the environment, time use, leisure and culture, democratic engagement, and living standards.

I understand that the purpose of this investigation is to acknowledge the limitations of traditional economic metrics and encourage people to think creatively about the complex factors influencing a good life, and encourage an innovative approach that could inform provincial priority-setting and long-term planning.

I haven't seen the instrument (apparently I have a one-in-five chance of getting it in the mail this month), but I'm told that toward the end of the thirty-minute survey, a few ambitious, overarching, soul-searching questions are asked. Questions such as: "Are the things you do in your life worthwhile?" and/or "How satisfied are you with your life in general?"

Regarding the indicators of the well-being of our province, apparently the CEO of *Engage Nova Scotia* believes that some non-traditional, non-economic indicators need to be identified and quantified. *If we treasure it, we should measure it,* is the mantra. This refrain has some poetic appeal, and it may even be true. I'm not sure.

Of course, it's a good thing for *Engage Nova Scotia* to call attention to the components of a good life that do not involve bank accounts, consumer price indices, debt-to-GDP ratios, and unemployment statistics. Gathering a comprehensive picture of how Nova Scotians are doing in areas that matter to them is a laudable undertaking. And in an age when data is bought and sold, mined and minted, and treated as a commodity, it is not surprising that we want to measure the things we value.

But for me, the measure-it-if-you-treasure-it rule doesn't ring true. I am not a data analyst or a scientist, but I understand both of these groups like to distinguish between qualitative measures and quantitative measures. Qualitative data tends to be subjective, gathered through interviews and surveys, described verbally, not amenable to numerical analysis.

It appears that since *Engage Nova Scotia* is attempting to gather qualitative data (inimical to numerical analysis), there exits an inherent inconsistency. Economists are famous for distorting data with the recondite language surrounding correlations, regressions, and normal distributions. Numerical data is drawn to this language. Caution is indicated.

And I'm pretty sure *Engage Nova Scotia* is interested in the determinants and antecedents of a quality life. I suspect these may be difficult to document.

No one I have encountered in recent days can specifically identify the behaviours and attitudes of those who seem content with their lives, but I have, in an earlier time, known a number of older people who seemed to have some idea.

Reflecting on their outlook and demeanor may inform discussions around the components of a quality life and the nature of happiness. If they were only still with us, old guys could help with the analysis.

My meager contribution to this bold project is to imagine responses from the senior citizens I knew before I became one. My commentary is based on the generation previous to mine—folks who are mostly dead and not in a position to challenge my claims. This confers more latitude.

Old folks tend to agree with the often repeated yet durable claim that *during good times, things are not as good as they appear to be, and during bad times, things are not as bad as they seem.* They seemed to think it best to keep the bigger picture in mind––at least to the extent that the exigencies of life will allow.

Life was best for those who kept an unexcited, steady hand on the tiller and advocated for a longer-term view, one less overwhelmed by the demands of the here and now. And although the old folks seemed happy in a quiet, understated way, it wasn't clear if happiness was the test for well-being at all—at least not the short-term variety of happiness that arrives unexpectedly and leaves just as quickly. These people didn't spend a lot of time contemplating their own personal drama.

For some, happiness was looked on with suspicion; it sounded too much like gratification, which seemed to involve taking pleasure, not dispersing it. They thought, maybe it's not really happiness we should be pursuing at all, but something far more nuanced, a blend of the satisfactions of good health, the contentment of achievement through effort, the peaceful consolations of an examined life, the splendors of nature, the appreciation of art and literature, service to others, connection to community, the affections of family and friends, and the continuity of the generations.

And those with years accumulating around them are blessed if they have a chance to enjoy the privileged satisfaction of growing old among people they love.

While there was no lack of ambition, the old guys seemed less concerned with glory or greatness and more with duty, responsibility, and necessity. A steady hand, a clear mind, a strong will—these will not only meet life's vicissitudes, they'll also make you feel good.

They didn't ask for much. The greatest joys life had to offer were not the result of unexpected good fortune (winning the lottery) but rather the restoration of the ordinary—a sick child returned to health, a destroyed barn rebuilt, a lost dog found, the return of the prodigal son. (*Dear God, Please know we are not asking for a golden goose; just put things back the way they were.*)

The old people encountered in my youth were not overly joyful or excessively gloomy. They never wasted time complaining about bad luck or lamenting a humdrum existence. Instead, they did what needed to be done and carried on. Self-esteem was the result of achievement, not a condition. Satisfaction was commensurate with effort expended. It wasn't dramatic self-sacrifice that was applauded, just steady, earnest exertion.

They seemed to take comfort in the habits and routines of their daily lives: the full-bellied contentment of Sunday dinner, hot coffee, cold beer, a new baby, a vigorous argument. Laughing at themselves and making fun of others seemed essential to human happiness.

And ordinary, repeated rituals––steaming tea and buttered toast every evening before bed, shining shoes on Saturday night, Sunday visitors––these small acts of ceremony helped to get them through. They seemed happy enough. Some were better at it than others. Often the satisfactions were not the direct result of recent fulfillments, but were experienced upon reflection, glorifying days looked back on.

I could easily be wrong about all this stuff, these maudlin sentiments distorted by time. Early-onset stupidity is a possibility as I sit here at my basement computer writing this questionable material.

My more reasonable wife is outside in the sunshine preparing her vegetable garden for planting. She's a worker. She's happy in the garden. I am reminded of a definition from Ambrose Bierce's dictionary (circa 1911): "CABBAGE, noun: A familiar garden vegetable about as large and as wise as a man's head."

Newspapers: An Elegy

Recently, a columnist with the SaltWire Network wrote a nostalgic article recalling his late father's love for newspapers, reminding us of the prominent place the paper-printed word occupied in the lives of previous generations, and the manner in which daily newspapers informed and enabled civic duty.

The story resonated with me. My own father (long deceased) was likewise enamoured with newspapers, almost excessively so, and spent part of his working life writing and reporting for the *Saint John Telegraph-Journal* during the early 1950s. And at home every evening, he consumed at least every word of two regional newspapers, clipped the articles of interest, and filed them in recycled, dog-eared manila file folders.

The process was painstaking and tedious. He had to go to the kitchen cupboard, retrieve the scissors he used to cut my hair, cut out the chosen articles neatly around the perimeter, paperclip detached portions together (if they continued on a second page), and walk upstairs to entomb them in his rusted file cabinet, where they were meticulously sorted by topic. Anyone in our house who dared to extract a clipping without replacing it exactly where it belonged had no interest in leading a long or happy life.

In my parents' room, jammed in beside their bed, my father had a small desk, whose surface was mostly taken up by an ancient gooseneck lamp and black Underwood manual typewriter that I could barely lift. The *e* key was worn out and illegible on the paper, the worn ribbon was black and red, and a stout little finger was needed to hold down the shift key. Their bedroom was small. Dad could change the ribbon on the typewriter without getting out of bed.

In addition to writing for the *Telegraph-Journal,* my father occasionally cranked out a few articles for *The Family Herald,* the least glamorous of Canada's magazines.

The *Family Herald* was a non-glossy edition printed on newspaper stock, labelled as *Canada's National Farm Magazine* and, for a time, one of Canada's most popular magazines—especially in rural Canada, where all the sensible people lived.

It contained reports on weather, farm markets, care and feeding of livestock, gardening/parenting tips, husbandry/midwifery, weed killers, and a section, Just for Girls, which included needlecraft and quilting. (At one time Ernest Buckler and Lucy Maude Montgomery were contributors). My father wrote a few farm-related articles, but his career with *The Family Herald* ended prematurely. Among print consumers, demand for guidance on crop rotation, slaughtering cattle, and greasing the hay baler contracted. *The Family Herald* died in 1968. Rural folk were pissed.

What a mistake it would be to imagine that those like my father, who dinged the carriage return bell, grappled with jammed keys, re-used carbon paper, and filed yellowed newspaper clippings, were churlish or naïve. Lots of folks from his generation did it. Those dog-eared clippings were not filed by fools or fanatics.

The current generation (including my children) consume news in ways that I don't even understand. Information is available from a thousand sources, credibility is difficult to discern, competition is fierce, and detail is determined by budget.

In the ongoing battle to generate content, print newspapers should remember (notwithstanding evidence south of the border) that words have meaning, truth matters, good taste and civility still have relevance. Free speech also matters, and I'm pretty sure no one has the absolute right to go through life without being offended.

And, as a guiding principle, print newspapers should not forget the wonderful, insightful Irish bartender *Mr. Dooley* (created by Finley Peter Dunne) who reminded us that "the job of the newspaper *is to comfort the afflicted and afflict the comfortable."*

At the end of his article, the author invited feedback. I haven't much to offer, except for a couple of images that I find both compelling and heartening:

Those wonderful pictures of the newsboys of the golden age of print in the early twentieth century, when every single day the great newspapers of the world churned out sixty to seventy pages (morning and evening editions) and sold them on the street for two cents. And every public library had the dailies available on a stick.

The idealized image of old-time newsrooms and editorial summits, where a diverse group of assertive, intelligent, thoughtful people got together every morning and discussed, debated, and disputed what was accurate, what was important, and where content should be located. (I assume something like this still occurs; thoughtful deliberation of this nature seems like a good thing.)

And the durable images of my father (like most of his generation), sitting in his big chair, reading the paper, hidden behind the pages, his big, freckled Irish hands and ink-smudged fingers on either side of the broadsheet, smiling, chortling, cursing quietly, oblivious to the household, absorbed in the print, rattling the pages—a man of strong opinions, exercising what he thought was his civic duty to stay informed throughout the length of his days.

These images are good. And as printed newspapers are threatened, we should remember them. Push back against the age.

Scanning the Obits

It's well known that it's mostly older folks who tend to read the obituaries, checking to see if anyone they know (or used to know) is gone, and to make sure their own name is not there among the departed, looking for confirmation that they are still alive in spite of the way they've been ignored lately at the walk-in clinic.

The melancholy perusal of the obits is generally a gloomy undertaking, but it can be leavened for those who come across an update on the current status of an adversary or a creditor. These folks can be mourned with restraint and moderation. And thoughtful readers will admit that any accounting of the sad and sobering business of dying occasionally has some entertainment value.

Not the least of which is (in this newspaper) the prolific and innovative nicknames by which the deceased were known, and their families affectionately feel compelled to mention. There are countless examples, but scanning the *Chronicle Herald* only as far back as the crane collapse during Hurricane Dorian's vandalism in Halifax, affectionate aliases like these have warmed the obituary columns: Bub, Bing, Peach, Cackie, Hubba, Heckie, Tubby, Amby, Super Woman, Jimmie the Waiter, and many more.

And it's no wonder the rural population of Nova Scotia is in decline. It appears that urban density advocates are getting their way. Living in the country must be bad for your health. On some days, it looks like everyone who dies in Nova Scotia is from a rural community.

For me at least, the obits contain regular geography lessons. Just recently, I had to go googling to find the location of Gibson Woods (near Kentville), Hectanooga (near Yarmouth), and Forties (near New Ross).

The same obituaries provide evidence that traditional church funerals are endangered, in our *enlightened* age replaced by celebrations of life, memorial services, or nothing at all.

At a traditional funeral, the ceremony is prescribed by religious rite and custom, an ordained celebrant presides, and the body of the deceased is present. The celebration of life is less restrictive and open to innovation. It may include singing and bright colours. Everyone in the room is alive. Monty Python's classic "Always Look on the Bright Side of Life" is often requested.

And in the light of older days, when people were *waked* at home or in the local church hall, for those of a certain age the scene is easy to recall: the dead at the far end of the room, friends congregated in groups of two or three, talking in low voices, staring at the floor, ignoring the casket, the men talking about the weather and feeling the obligation to console themselves after the funeral (two pints should do), the women commenting on the deceased, how nice she looks, and what a lovely job they made of laying her out.

And a tight-collared, red-faced priest is circulating, dispensing prayers and praise. *Sorry for your troubles.* He goes to a corner of the room to console a little woman hiding behind a prayer book, sobbing, her nose in bloom. *Blessed are they who mourn, for they shall be comforted.* In the kitchen, there is a gallon of tea and a boatload of cut sandwiches (no crusts).

And if, during the standing-around portion of the wake, you could position yourself to eavesdrop on two older ladies of the parish, their back-and-forth dialogue could provide insight into the character of the deceased.

"Ah, poor Dorothy. She made a lovely corpse."

"Yes, but toward the end, she put some weight on."

"And I didn't think she'd ever stop talking."

"Well, she's quiet enough just now."

"Yes, the poor thing, she'll be dead a long time."

No one should speak ill of the dead. That's the law. And everyone knows when it comes to the character of the deceased, funerals cause correction. The life of the grieved does not always typify the virtues mourned. Faults become ingratiating faults. Weaknesses become redeeming weaknesses. Ordinary people sprout wings. Sinners mutate into exemplars of virtue. Uncle Albert, previously profane, is now a latter-day saint. Cranky old Aunt Teresa becomes Mother Teresa. We can expect her beatification immediately after the interment.

And the cemetery, whistled past, provides a range of epitaphs, most of them solemn and thoughtful, but occasionally offering additional entertainment. My favourite inscription is the poetic instruction from a grieving wife who was unworried about her husband's legacy: *Mourners pause, but shed no tear. It's a horse's arse that lieth here.*

I read somewhere that a child's earliest memories often include their first encounter with a body in a coffin, usually a relative. It may be so.

My grandmother died when I was in elementary school. Sixty years ago at her wake, my mother directed my sister and me to be quiet and respectful. We should not be frightened when we saw the body laid out in the living room. My mother explained that we would be going to the funeral and burial tomorrow morning. She cautioned that we might find the casket lowered into the ground disturbing. She would throw a shovelful of dirt. *Dust to dust*, she explained, *from whence we came*. I can remember I had a question about putting dead people in the ground and covering them with dirt, but I knew I shouldn't mention it.

During the wake that evening, my sister and I were praying (at least kneeling) directly in front of the open coffin within arm's length of Grammy's wrinkled face. I wanted to reach in and take off her wire-rimmed glasses—they seemed to me unnecessary.

Grammy was pale. I examined her face closely and imagined her in the ground with worms crawling up her nose. I knew this was wrong. I shouldn't be thinking of worms in Grammy's nose, but I couldn't help it. She had a black rosary (with the paint worn off the beads) entwined around her white, bony fingers.

When my sister and I completed our benediction, we blessed ourselves and bolted for the kitchen. Grammy stayed in the living room, at peace, resting. The large kitchen table was loaded with egg sandwiches with the crusts cut off, molasses cookies, and cold milk. There was an empty rocking chair at the end of the table.

After the First World War, reflecting *on short-term vs. long-term economic policy,* and with the profound insight only available to economists, John Maynard Keynes famously noted that *in the long run, we are all dead*. People even smarter than Keynes believe that, occasionally, we should think about the common fate that unites us.

If this is good advice, I'll invoke the great Irishman Oscar Wilde: *The best thing I can do with good advice is pass it along. It's of no use to me."*

GETTING OUT OF THE HOUSE

Carnivores and Other Sinners

Citing a recent study, the *Chronicle Herald* reported this week that an increasing number of Canadians are reducing their meat intake. The study indicates that folks like me are in the demographic (older male boomers) least likely to diminish the pleasures of the (animal) flesh. This fact may assuage any guilt I have regarding my meaty dining habits, which I wasn't feeling too bad about in the first place.

On the basis of no dietary knowledge or expertise whatsoever, I want to weigh in.

I'm pretty sure that it's a good idea to moderate processed meat intake, but I'm skeptical about the pessimism surrounding meat consumption overall. My skepticism is based on two factors: The historical record of dependence on meat as a source of protein, and because I enjoy eating it so much.

Consuming too much meat is on my list of the things I do but shouldn't, a list now into a third page, single spaced. I will oppose any plans to replace wing nite at our local pub with kelp-and-tofu nite, even if every order includes an avocado on the side. I remain a beef apologist, a mercenary in the protein war. My favourite animal is steak.

And I feel a debt of gratitude to the beef farmers that feed my habit. These farmers are thankful for good weather and thankful that they can work seven-day weeks. And I'm thankful I'm not a farmer. My grandfather kept cattle and throughout his lifetime (a period when hash was made from corned beef and potatoes, and pot was where you cooked the stew). He was delighted to hoe into a roast beef anytime it was available, even if it came from cows he had known personally, or helped birth, or nursed back to health. He had no qualms about eating pork rinds at breakfast, even those with a few hairs in them. Gravy on buttered potatoes didn't seem excessive.

To bolster my argument for beef sovereignty, I offer (instead of logic and reason) a transformational dining experience that will assuage the mind of even the most ardent kelp lovers, and convert meatless heretics––at least those willing to set aside dietary resolutions and weight restrictions––back to the faith. Here's how the pilgrimage works:

One day this week, skip lunch and then go to the MicMac Tavern for supper and order a rib steak. The smallest size on the menu is eighteen ounces. By any reasonable standard, an eighteen ounce rib steak is excessive, unnecessary, and gluttonous.

It is also a gift from God. Consumption is a spiritual experience that will change you profoundly, more deeply than a trip to India or a visit to the legislature in session. Religious men have considered the consumption of wine a religious experience ever since the wedding feast at Cana. Such is the rib-steak at the MicMac.

After the first few bites, first-timers are overcome; they have reached a turning point in life, the souls awakening. They pause, gaze at their plate reverently, and speak in whispers. One should not be too quick to condemn dietary fervor of this type. It is a solemn occasion not to be trifled with.

At the end of their rib-steak meal, customers take the last swig of their draft beer and are content. All is well with the world. Sometimes they begin to purr.

In Nova Scotia, meat lovers of Scottish heritage know Robbie Burns was a meat enthusiast. When asked to say grace in Kirkcudbright, at a dinner given by the Earl of Selkirk, Burns offered the now-famous Selkirk Grace. Meat is the central theme.

> *Some hae meat and canna eat,*
> *And some wad eat that want it,*
> *But we hae meat and we can eat,*
> *Sae let the Lord be Thankit!*

I'm with Burns. *Let the Lord be thankit.*

Wing Night

If you're eating chicken wings, the chances are you're someplace where people are having a good time. They don't serve wings at funerals, state dinners, or PTA meetings.

And if pub-patrons are gnawing on wings, it's a safe bet that there's cold beer nearby and more on the way. It's probably Thursday around suppertime, and the pub's population is, at least temporarily, content with the world.

About once a week, my wife and I go to a local pub for wings, usually with our friends Albert and Theresa. In our local saloon, the clientele constitute an agreeable cross-section of our community, groups of friends and families, all types, all ages. There are ball caps, business suits, hockey jerseys, emblemed leather jackets, children in high chairs, and at least one older woman using a walker. These are ordinary neighbourhood folks, robust and well-rounded, plain, pierced, patched, wrinkled, ironed, tattooed. And to make me feel better, there's always a lot of white hair and shiny heads, and men going to the bathroom, moving slowly. There are well-groomed patrons wiping wing-sauce (mild, medium, or hot) from the shirt sleeve, and bilingual Nova Scotians who speak both English and profanity. Not all of the food served here is recommended by Healthy Heart Association or your family doctor. These are generous people untroubled by kale, kelp, or calories. There are not many vegetarians or librarians. The menu provides a diet that only thins your hair. The ambiance has a pleasing communal feel to it.

We're met at the door by two girls on a local sports team selling tickets in support of their next trip to God Knows Where (and in a few minutes we'll meet their mother making the table rounds with a white bucket selling 50/50 tickets). Some regulars are perched at the bar or roosting at the high tables on the far side. Most of the tables are filled, except the one next to us where folks are saving chairs for a group joining them later. When the latecomers arrive, everyone gets up and hugs everyone else. Men my age are confused by this convention; we wonder when, and by whose authority, this irritating hugging habit got itself established. For us it's a mystery, like why people eat soybeans, or read whatever Oprah tells them to.

Over the next hour my friend Albert will have three beers and ten wings; it never varies. He calls it a four-course meal. During the meal he gets up to go to the bathroom at least once. Albert tells us he doesn't really have to go, but when you're over sixty-five it's required by law. Every week Albert tells us the same joke ... *did you know that in Quebec St. Hubert is the patron saint of fried chicken?*

Wing-eating is not an elegant experience. We are released from formality and the obligations of refined dining. We use a lot of napkins. Daintiness and sophistication don't really come into play. We eat with our hands, we suck the meat off the skeleton, and we throw the detritus in a plastic basket.

There is a young family sitting at the table beside us. Mom and dad are pleasant and robust––about four hundred pounds of solid parenting––with healthy looking kids. As they wait for their order, mom is teaching the kids how to use an iPhone. Her husband is searching for an entry point into the conversation. Mom knows what she is talking about. I am impressed by her depth, as well as her width.

When the order arrives, everyone hoes into the wings and the whole family is tossing bones into the same basket. A skeletal mound is rising, like Buffalo Jump; the kids can hardly see over the top of it. It's very impressive––maybe not enough for the Guinness book, but still pretty remarkable. You can just see the tops of their heads.

A couple of tables away there's a guy, not fastidious in his dining habits, enjoying fried clams. We can hear him eat. He is tilting his head back and slurping down clams like a seagull eating a mackerel. No one minds this behaviour; this is the land of carefree imperfections, the land of grease and salt and cold beer on tap. The servers are wonderful, energetic, friendly and attentive to our needs (*How are things tasting so far? Another beer?*).

It seems that at most Nova Scotia pubs, wing-nite is usually on Thursday, and hardly ever on Friday.

This is because of the Catholics. Under a papal embargo, previous generations of Roman Catholic beer drinkers ate only fish on Friday. Eating meat from any warm-blooded animal was not only illegal, but punishable by slow-roasting in hell. These days nobody understands (or pays any attention to) the meat-eating prohibition, but I was lucky enough to have Sister Donovan explain it to me when I was in grade four. She told me that because Christ died on Good Friday, the consumption of all warm-blooded flesh is prohibited as a gesture of solidarity. Fish is acceptable because all species of fish are cold-blooded––as are amphibians, criminal lawyers, and free-market economists.

In any case, this is why wing-nite is on Thursday and not on Friday, because of the Pope and Sister Donovan. (The Irish used to pay particular attention to the meat-eating prohibition. When a Dublin mother learned that her son, travelling in Africa, had been eaten by cannibals, she was distraught when she checked the calendar and found he was eaten on a Friday. "And during lent!" she wailed.)

Apparently the habit of eating chicken wings is only about fifty years old, originating in Buffalo New York, at a time when wings were considered the throwaway part of the chicken with the same status as liver and pig knuckles

Ever since Teressa Bellissimo first served up wings at The Anchor Bar in Buffalo, poultry producers' parts departments have struggled to maintain their inventory. Chickens have been caught in an economic updraft. The confluence of several factors––cheap protein, pub-custom, football mania, gourmet spices, flat screen TVs, craft beers, working class solidarity, and popular debauchery–– have resulted in a weekly ritual more popular then Sunday Mass. Our culture has been changed; an entire wing-centered social structure has emerged. Chicken producers are happy, prices are on the rise, demand is soaring––most of the wind is beneath the wings.

Notwithstanding the burgeoning demand, pub-patrons need not worry about wing-scarcities. Wing-regeneration research is underway. Here's how it works.

It is well known that some insurance lizards (such as geckos) can discard one or more of their appendages (usually a tail) when attacked by a predator, and then re-grow a new one when they are left alone at the office. This capacity for tail-regeneration––called autotomy––provides the basis for the resolution of the wing-shortage dilemma. Geneticists are developing a type of chicken-autotomy that would allow wings to be clipped from live chickens that have the ability to regrow them in a couple of weeks.

You can see how this would be helpful. These improvements are happening in the labouratory right next door to where biologists are cloning a boneless pig made entirely of maple-smoked bacon. And down the hall, in a room with no chairs, a standing committee of nutritionists has been working for years on *The Milk Question* ("Is it good for us, or not?"). The inexorable advancement of science is a wonderful thing.

I have a friend who keeps a single pet chicken in the backyard. The chicken's name is Orville Wright. Orville can only fly a few feet before she has to land, but to her credit, Orville just keeps on trying, and is convinced that long distance flight is in her future. Orville is plagued by vestigial dreams of her ancestors, the jungle fowl who flew high into the trees to roost. These days Orville is getting old and rarely takes flight, unless she is startled by someone resembling Colonel Sanders or Mary Brown.

Orville is a sensitive bird who knows that in the local pub her wings are worth only about sixty cents each. She tries not to think about it.

QUESTIONABLE COMMENTARY

Eating Out

I have a friend who maintains that retirement is often squandered on people who still want to work. This may be true in some cases, but mostly it's just prattle coming from those of us who claim to miss the workplace but know full well that retirement has much to recommend it—especially the not-having-to-go-to-work part.

Retirees have benefits: In addition to discounts and parking spaces, it turns out we don't need to care nearly as much about what other people think, we hardly ever have to buy new shoes, and as the years accumulate, many of the people we never really cared for show up in the obituaries. Even better, as we get older, we can eat in restaurants far more often than we used to.

I suspect there is a whole category of seniors like my wife and me who had limited restaurant experience prior to retirement, when we were busy with working lives and children, not to mention the budget restraints and austerity programs. In those days, if we went out at all it was usually someplace with institutional lighting and oversized calendars on the wall. In particular, we have fond memories of the Irving Big Stops and their hot chicken sandwiches, three inches thick, with fries and canned peas and thick gravy over everything, including the laminated menu.

In our dotage, my wife and I are inclined to go out to eat more frequently than we should. With our friends Albert and Theresa, we normally indulge this inclination in Dartmouth area restaurants. In the old days, the hot chicken was great, but when the children leave home and the mortgage is paid off, we sometimes feel like eating in a place where the men take their hats off.

Except to confess that I have an eating disorder involving an unhealthy (but loving) relationship with the rib steak at the MicMac Tavern, I'll leave it to Bill Spurr and other professional reviewers to comment on specific restaurants and to apply the recondite adjectives (puckish, wry, ambrosial) related to the tart/savory/smoky entrées and the crumbly/crunchy/creamy desserts. No food reviews from me (suffice it to say that in almost every case, our eating-out experience is agreeable, and meals surprisingly good).

In particular, those of us in declining vitality admire the ability and energy of the servers, who are most often females. The young lady who served our table on Friday evening provided a typical and worthy example of the competent service to which we have grown accustomed. She easily managed the delicate but essential balance of friendliness and efficiency. Most impressive was her energy level. She moved quickly and efficiently, bopping around from table to table, multitasking at unsafe speeds. Albert says, "She was jumping around like a rabbit on his first date."

And no matter which restaurant we choose, we welcome the standardized routines and the predictability. As soon as you walk in the door, a pleasant woman greets you, seats you, menus you, offers drinks, and recites the daily specials with flawless precision. She is nimble in the art of napkin/cutlery distribution. Water and wine glasses are attended to. The women order Merlot, Albert and I get a beer, Irish Red. (Ben Franklin was right; beer is proof that God loves us and wants us to be happy). We peruse the menu (*take your time, there's no rush*) and order the meals. The sunny young lady doesn't write anything down and makes an impression on patrons who can't remember where they parked. We wait for our supper and have a look around.

The place is busy, a drone of conversations. On the other side there is a loud talker. Every restaurant has one, the guy who knows a lot about everything and feels an obligation to share with all others in the room. Beside him, a lovely young family is sharing a meal, all four of them swiping their phones. And at the table right next to us, a cranky woman, who could be mistaken for Angela Merkel, has called our server over to complain about a water stain on her knife. The server apologizes and replaces it with cheerful indifference and gets busy with the rest of her duties. Merkel examines the new knife and scowls, overcome by the weight of her existence. Her husband, not a sparkling conversationalist, looks like a guy who had better not leave a tea bag in the sink.

The meal arrives exactly as ordered. A polite young lady asks would we like some fresh pepper. She brings over a four-foot grinder and twists the top with some effort, like she was opening a cathedral door. Maybe there are some nuances of peppercorn grinding I don't comprehend, but it seems to me that those things are excessively large. In this case the poor girl could hardly lift it. If that pepper grinder and Danny DeVito were standing side by side, it would be hard to tell which was which. We were grateful for her efforts. The pepper was very fresh, although a bit spicy.

Our server is busy attending to tables all around us, but just as my first morsel of pan-fried haddock hovers in mid-air between my plate and my mouth, she drops by to ask how everything tastes so far. All I've sampled so far is the Irish Red, so I assure her that everything tastes great. During the next twenty minutes she checks in on us several more times. At the exact moment any one of us is done eating, she appears from nowhere to take away the empty plate, even though the rest of us are still chomping away and don't require any additional table space. This instantaneous dish removal convention, practiced at all restaurants in the Western hemisphere, is one of those things I can't understand, like why there are so many pillows on our couch. There must be a shortage of plates in the kitchen.

When we are done, there is nothing left on my plate except those hard vegetables (all shiny and shellacked) which I assume have an aesthetic, rather than a nutritional, purpose. Our wives reminisce about the days when people used to cook vegetables. The rest of the dishes are cleared. The women have desert and Albert and I order an Irish coffee. Albert tells the story about his parish priest (Father O'Brien) who, although he took a vow of chastity, always consummates his evening meal with Irish coffee––made with Jameson, the Catholic whiskey, distilled in the Republic.

Our effervescent server comes by with the bill and the debit machine. As I am punching in the numbers, she pleasantly asks "any plans for the evening?" (On Friday, a variation of this inquiry is "any plans for the weekend?"). To her credit, she makes it sound like she really cares about our calendar of weekend social events. We have noted that in restaurants throughout the metro area, the business of passing the debit machine to the customer provokes this same inquiry. The any-plans-for-the-weekend question may seem a bit personal and intrusive, but I assume it is required by law, or the food server's code of behaviour. You can't blame the server; she's just following the rules. She's at the end of an eight-hour shift, on her feet the whole time.

As we leave, her enthusiasm has not diminished and she thanks us with a big smile. She deserves a much bigger tip than I give her. I don't know why I held back. I'm old and confused, I'm concerned about my triglyceride levels, and I have no plans for the weekend.

CHEWING THE RAG

Sense and Humour

I have no direct or personal affiliation with John Crosby, but when he died earlier this year, I shared with thousands of Canadians a sense of loss. Not only for his enduring contributions to Newfoundland and Canada but more so for the loss of an invigorating personality, the loss of a man of character, the loss of a man whose humour and humanity were fully revealed.

In an age when the indignation industry is flourishing, the market value of candid humour is under pressure. I worry that Crosby's species is endangered. I secretly fear that my Newfoundland neighbour is right; that *the likes of him will not be seen again*. When Crosby died, the media generously enumerated deeds and duties, accolades and tributes. But the inventory of Crosby's considerable accomplishments was only a preamble to the description of his candor, jocularity, wit, and impressive range of profanity and poetic insults. Our affections and recollections of Crosby coalesce around his wit. We remember John Crosby because his humanity and humour were right there in front of us. It strikes me as peculiar that not many politicians seem to understand this.

Among colleagues and acquaintances (especially seniors) in our broader social networks, the suggestion that one among us has *no sense of humour* is not an uncommon reproach, but it is, oddly, among the worst of aspersions we can cast. To some extent, we forgive many human shortcomings—personality defects, baldness, early-onset stupidity, various warts and wrinkles—but grim humourlessness is unpardonable. Describing someone as lacking a sense of humour is a serious disparagement. It deprives them of all other agreeable attributes. No sensible person should willingly admit to being without one.

Albert is a good man, we say, *honourable and upright, but it's such a shame he has no sense of humour.* Thus is Albert divested of all other virtues; his noble qualities are annulled, his decency is voided, his respectability is negated. Albert's merits cannot emerge from the shadow of his ominous gloom. His humourlessness has veto power.

Older people recognize that a properly cultivated sense of humour includes elements of humility and self-deprecation. Making fun of ourselves allows us to be more agreeable to each other. They also understand that the benefit of not *taking-ourselves-too-seriously* needs to be nurtured. Personal weaknesses and shortcomings are useful in this way. They have therapeutic value. (If you have trouble enumerating your own inadequacies, you can always find a friend who is willing to help.)

Humour takes people's minds off themselves and their personal drama. Folks who don't take themselves too seriously are more willing to forgive others, to tolerate weakness, to accept frailty. The virtue-signaling feature of moral indignation doesn't sit well with them. The self-congratulating part makes them uncomfortable.

Generally, laughter and hatred are estranged; their cohabitation is awkward. Even a personal insult, if clever and well delivered, can be forgiven if it's funny enough. If it's *a good one*, it's less likely to motivate revenge. A lot of effort is required to dislike anyone who makes you laugh.

As has often been noted, humour is an important part of what makes us human. I>m told that a few other species make laughing sounds (sort of), and a few are thought to appreciate humour (sort of), but apparently it's only the human species (except office managers and cabinet ministers) who laugh out loud.

The humour sense is deemed to be (like everything else) worthy of academic scrutiny. Some deep thinkers believe that lack of this sense indicates weak character and poor mental health (this could be true––think POTUS, bleakness his birthright). Others suggest that the humour sense, the ubiquitous phenomenon enjoyed by every age and every culture, may mutate slightly among older populations. The internet is lumpy with *getting-old* jokes and cartoons. Like a virus, they disperse among seniors at an exponential rate. Seniors comprehend the necessity for humour.

Although they look at the solemn and the serious with suspicion, seniors understand that when something is funny, they should have a second look at it for insight, for embedded truth.

They tend to notice the foolishness of priorities, the absurdity of life. They are comfortable with flaws and follies. They are more likely to suffer fools gladly because they feel at home among them. Seniors choose laughter over despair to mitigate their own physical deterioration. With everyone sitting around the departure lounge, someone might as well tell a story; although it's a nimble art, humour can easily migrate into nostalgia and melancholy.

Seniors tell the same stories over and over, and laugh every time––the tale is often not as funny as the telling of it. Their jokes tend to be less aggressive, more deadpan, strewn with plenty of self-ridicule. (*An old man goes to his doctor complaining about an arthritic back, so bad he can't bend over to tie his shoes. The doctor says, "how flexible are you?" The man says, "I can't come on Tuesdays."*). Not bad, but not as good as this one my friend Albert repeats at regular intervals.

Albert's brother-in-law (a fellow pensioner and fishing buddy) has a wife who is known to all of us as a chronic hypochondriac. Dorothy is convinced she has a responsibility to incubate every contagious disease as soon as it becomes available. Any condition of infirmity Dorothy is told about, she begins to notice the symptoms in herself. When someone complains about a ringing in their ears, Dorothy hears it too. If a neighbour is seeing spots in front of her eyes, Dorothy can see them as well.

One evening while we were sitting in the garage having a pint of plain, Dorothy's husband showed us a photograph of his wife standing on the porch of the lakeside log cabin he had recently purchased.

"It's a great place," he said proudly. "And there's Dorothy on the porch. She's the one with the shingles."

Surely folks who tell stories like this live longer than they would otherwise.

On more practical matters: Years ago, a friend of mine (himself rich in limitations) provided me his 3-H recipe for success in the workplace: *Humour, Humility, and Hard Work*. I think it's as good as any scholarly dissertation on leadership and organizational health. Humour is the first one.

Tim's Tidbits

Notwithstanding minimum-wage issues in Ontario and franchisee lawsuits in the US, there is ample evidence that Tim Hortons is doing well in Nova Scotia. The highways are littered with the data, caffeine lineups reach into the street, and coffee-related traffic congestion is commonplace. Mid-morning, if motorists come across a traffic slowdown they can't quite see the cause of, the chances are pretty good that up ahead they'll find a leisurely street-crossing pedestrian, a spandexed cyclist asserting his inalienable rights, or a vehicle turning left into Tim's. Such interruptions are often experienced by old guys heading out for ten o'clock coffee with fellow retirees. They are in no hurry and really don't mind the delay. There will be lots of time later to get in a nap before lunch.

These guys get together at Tim's once a week for coffee, doughnuts, and disputation. They spend an hour chewing the rag, commenting, remembering, ridiculing and arguing. Beyond their best days, they are observers of the world now, less participants. They are polite to the girls behind the counter, and they don't cause any trouble. They have bad backs and good spirits, and seem to be mellowed by the accumulation of years. At Tim's, these EONS (Elderly Ordinary Nova Scotians) constitute a chattering class of their own. An astute listener might find their conversations both entertaining and instructive. Their expertise, insight, and wisdom are worn lightly but worth paying attention to.

It is clear these guys consider the later years too important to be taken seriously. They are too old to be sure of themselves and have little patience for the complacent certainty shown by the towering intellects of academia. They have a broad range of interests and opinions, and although comments can be derisive and sardonic, they are neither strident nor malicious. They project an uncertain skepticism and caution regarding advanced thinkers and modern times. Their comic grievances and lamentations are wide ranging but current, generally based on the last reading of the *Chronicle Herald*. Next time you go for a coffee, sit quietly nearby and listen. You have to pay attention; they jump all over the place.

Here are some samples of extemporaneous musings. On dissolution of school boards: It may be good idea, but if inefficiency and public apathy provide the rationale, then all democratic institutions are at risk, certainly provincial governments. On Mount St. Vincent coarse assignments: Do I have to be an amoeba to teach biology? Should I take an ancient history course from a guy who is still alive? On doctor scarcity: Just pay them. On leaving the church: Take comfort where you can find it, but if orthodoxy requires you to suspend rational thought, run the other way. On universities: pious advocates of critical inquiry and subtle prohibitions on free speech. On harvesting old growth forests: We should stop doing that. On technology: Anyone interested in pursuing happiness may not want to spend their life staring at a smartphone. On our Prime Minister: We are worried he will run out of people to apologize to.

On social justice warriors: tolerant of everyone except those with another point of view. On the evening television news: nice people giggling about cats and dogs and recycled YouTube videos. On America and the decline of civilization: Reasonable people can debate free trade and immigration policies, but if you find yourself arguing about whether chaos is a legitimate approach to leadership, whether words have meaning, or whether truth matters, then all is lost.

These overheard timbits provide only a superficial glance into the expansive minds of EONS. They are capable of much deeper analysis. High-level discussions happen at Tim Hortons across our province, clearly an untapped resource. A study should be undertaken. If creativity can be an industry in Cape Breton, what about the vast storehouse of knowledge residing in the Tim Hortons think tanks?

On this day, the last discussion item was the declining empire to the south and Trump's thoughtful and eloquent response when he was recently asked about the prospects of nuclear war with North Korea (*We'll see*, the President articulated).

One guy had a doctor's appointment and had to leave early. The others (grinning) asked if it was anything serious because they wanted to know if they needed to save a chair for him next week. *Same as Trump*, he said. *We'll see*.

These guys recognize their limitations. They don't own a laptop, have never been to Starbucks, never tasted a latté. They are not on Bookface or Tweeter (sic) and they make no claims to the exclusions of ageism or the anxieties of social isolation. They are not looking for ways to be offended.

For the most part, they consider themselves lucky. They can extract wisdom from a range of sources, including Irish poets, German philosophers, and country singers. On the topic of old age and mortality, they prefer to ignore Dylan Thomas's advice to *rage against the dying of the light* in favour of Willie Nelson's grateful anthem, *I Woke up Still Not Dead Again Today*.

Contrarian's Summit

When our pod of retired contrarians got together last Tuesday morning for coffee at Tim Hortons, an extraordinary decision was reached—not unanimously, but with only one dissenting vote. After years of congregating weekly at Tim's, we decided on a change of venue. Albert, the most curmudgeonly of our group (opposed to all change, as a matter of principle) expressed his opposition, but agreed to go along with the consensus. Next Tuesday, it was decided upon, we would abandon Tim's and meet at the cafeteria at Ikea, where you can get a full breakfast for $2.85, with no assembly required. (In his dissenting opinion, Albert imagined that as you pushed your tray toward the utensil rack, you would have to pick up a knife and a fork and an Allen wrench)

In the end, Albert reluctantly agreed that, on a pension income, the enticement of a complete breakfast for less than three dollars was tough to resist. Also, there were free coffee refills.

This is bad news for Tim's which, already suffering from labour and legal turbulence, may not be able to recover from the revenue loss resulting from the exodus of retirees who have no trouble spending up to $1.79 (medium dark roast) every Tuesday morning. Beginnings next week, as the market becomes aware of our migration, expect pressure on stock value.

From now on, we will chew the rag in the cafeteria of the mountaintop Swedish Embassy and complete our comprehensive analysis of the news of the past week. No matter the venue, our lighthearted nattering stays about the same. Our scrutiny sometimes includes a breakdown of the prattle on network television (CNN is our favourite because it features the same breaking news every ten minutes, always right after the commercial), but mostly it's the news and opinions published in the *Chronicle Herald* that get a thorough vetting.

Last week, several disparate news items were mentioned only briefly. We touched on transatlantic flights, transgender washrooms, and trans-mountain pipelines, and whether permits issued by federal and provincial governments have any relevance. We feel pretty good now that we've become (due to our steel and aluminum exports) a national security threat to Trump's America. Since the war of 1812, it's our first time being a national security threat, although we fear it won't last long––as soon as Trump voters contemplate an impact on aluminum beer can production, tariffs will be withdrawn.

We touched on immigration policy and how dramatically the Nova Scotia economy would be improved (and the tick population depleted) if only wild turkeys were encouraged to colonize here. And we learned how many seniors fear running out of money before they die, and Albert (vulnerable but trying to make the best of it) pointed out that if you are going to run out of money, before you die is the time to do it. Running out after you die is hardly worth your while.

And what about those islands of plastic waste in the Pacific Ocean, some bigger than Ontario, and this includes the Greater Toronto Area?

None of these topics generated as much uneasiness among us as an early June article which relayed the disturbing news that Donald Trump's mother, Mary Anne MacLeod, was from the Outer Hebrides in northwestern Scotland. Trump's grandfather was a fisherman named Malcolm MacLeod, and his grandfather was Alexander McLeod (Alexander, Malcolm, Donald, cottages, thatched roofs, and crofters—sound familiar?). Trumps mother and maternal grandparents were Gaelic speakers.

This news is disconcerting. Several of us have Scottish ancestry. This news is like an Irish Republican getting back his DNA testing and finding out he is related to Oliver Cromwell. The article reports that the pioneers of Judique and Mabou are not anxious to claim a connection to Trump. Maybe after the Impeachment, if Rodney MacDonald will allow it, Trump could enroll at the Gaelic College so he can learn his mother tongue and step dancing. Admission could be part of the CMFTA Agreement. He could host a kitchen ceilidh and invite his best friends Kim and Vladimir.

Toward the end of our session, as we were finishing up the third coffee refill, the discussion returned to our Prime Minister. Albert expressed his admiration, pointing out what a malleable young man he was, able to adjust (like the Vicar of Brae) with ease and simplicity to his current geography and circumstance. Opposed to oil pipelines in the east, he is able to amend his point of view as he approaches the Alberta border. Opposed to fossil fuel incentives in Paris, he's okay with them in Calgary. Just a couple of months after enthusiastically signing the Paris Agreement on Climate Change, Mr. Trudeau bought us a pipeline, using our credit card.

Albert said he always wanted to be in the oil business but suggested that Mr. Trudeau should be cautioned about his inconsistent behaviour and the dangers of adaptation. He explained that creatures constantly attempting to acclimatize to their immediate environment can find themselves in difficulty. He told us the story of the exotic pet owner who, in an effort to keep his chameleon warm on a cold morning, wrapped it in Scottish tartan. The poor thing died of exhaustion.

Of course, we are not sure of any of this. We are just old guys talking. If historian Will Durant was right when he said *education is the progressive discovery of our ignorance*, then you have no worries. Within our group, our education is progressing nicely.

QUESTIONABLE COMMENTARY

Observations from the Corner Booth

It was the great Yankee Hall-of-Famer Yogi Berra who once explained to the rest of the world that "you can observe a lot just by watching," and since that time, there seems to be some consensus that you can also hear a lot just by listening. And it turns out that the knowledge gleaned can come from unexpected sources. These diverse sources include almost any Tim Hortons restaurant in Nova Scotia at around 10:00a.m. on weekday mornings. There you'll usually find a gaggle of retired guys sitting together for coffee.

Often I am part of such a gaggling group. Other times I inadvertently find myself sitting alone with my back to an adjacent booth populated by geezers unknown to me, but (after a few minutes of eavesdropping) prove similar in spirit and disposition. Such was the case on Tuesday this week. I am sitting with my back to three seniors in seminar. Two of them are around seventy I'd guess, but the third is older and shakier––must be about eighty-five. They are all in high spirits, happy to be above ground, on the green side of the turf, sitting in front of a medium-double-double and a doughnut. The lads have a lot to say to each other, and I can hear every word of it. They couldn't care less if I'm listening or not. (I'll get back to these guys in a minute.)

First, an inventory of Tim's patrons:

At the table over by the recycle station, there are two young women, among the noblest of God's creatures, one dressed as a successful small business owner, the other sporting an Adidas jacket, the splendor of purple spandex, ear buds, and a Fitbit. They are carrying on a weighty discussion while drinking green tea (no milk) and extoling the virtues of a plant-based diet. They use words like *passionate* and *excited*. One takes a delicate sip and begins to describe the sincerity and scope of her concern for meat-eaters and other reprobates. She is passionate about raising the consciousness, but it is delicate work. They are obviously close friends, united in vegetarian fervour. "Why don't you come for supper tonight?" one of them says. "We're having couscous and kelp casserole." Yum. Followed, I assume, by a quiet evening of meditation and travelling inward.

At the far end of the restaurant, a clutch of half dozen teenagers (skipping school, I guess––10:00a.m. on Tuesday) crowd into a booth. They seem different from the other customers. Some are carrying textbooks. Their demeanor and speech patterns are different. For the most part, they're ignoring each other.

Their universe is illuminated not by the sun, but by the light from small screens.

Among this group, at the end of the bench facing me, is a low-spirited, backward-ball-capped scholar, a lad of about sixteen or seventeen. Slouching under the weight of his existence, he can barely stay awake, or lift the weight of his iPhone 11Pro. The young man does not appear to have a head seething with ideas. In younger days, he may have been deprived of the satisfactions of work. The script guiding his behaviour seems to be as follows: ignore everything in the immediate environment, accept the burdens of a callous and capricious world, and swipe left. The lad has on a designer red T-shirt with bold lettering across the front that proclaims his Irish heritage in Gaelic font, and sums up the hopes and dreams of his adolescence. *Pog mo thoin*, it says, a fine broth of a boy he is––clearly a Republican.

At a nearby table (next to the passionate women with the green tea) is a robust middle-aged couple. Each has an extra-large coffee and two Boston Crème doughnuts on a plate. It's not their first time sitting behind a plate of doughnuts. Both are bulky.

She is a well-dressed, broad-beamed, ample breasted woman with two eyes and three chins. She is wearing a tight sweater and an industrial-strength bra. Her man is also dressed in his Sunday best, with a red tie and a blue blazer, double breasted like his wife. They are chatting away, getting along like a pair of old shoes. The woman in particular seems high spirited. She has a warm smile and a very pleasant face (although three chins seems excessive).

Let's get back to the old guys. None of the other patrons are paying the slightest attention to them. Old men know that they can be invisible in public places. They see this as liberating. Nobody bothers them. They talk about sports and politics, people they used to know, what's for supper, and laundry. Sometimes they talk about the places where they used to work, but only to each other. They understand obsolescence. They know no one really cares. They have learned the overarching lessons: a lot of what you thought was important, isn't, and a lot of the things you thought mattered, don't. These guys are familiar with the pretenses of the world.

They are filled with age and doubt, thinking it good if everyone had reliable friends, a reasonable pension, and regular bowel movements.

Their conversation lurches from topic to topic, punctuated with soft-spoken profanity, not meant to impress. They don't take themselves too seriously and aren't sure of anything, but they do have opinions, points of view that, on the face, may appear trivial but on closer scrutiny may be worth considering. The following examples were distilled from my eavesdropping.

On the constituents of a decent meal: "… salt cod and scrunchions (ya can't beat it with a stick), possibly followed by a wee nip from the jar." On Meghan and Harry: "… my interest in royalty is limited to Dukes of Hazzard and the Queen of Hearts." On progressive thinkers: "… they confuse an open mind with an empty mind." On a couple in the corner, now rutting and clutching: "… turn a hose on them."

On God: "… maybe he exists and maybe he doesn't, how the hell am I supposed to know." On Bill Gates' bank account: "… that guy there has more money than you and I put together." On high fashion: "… Donegal tweed and Aran wool." On minor pleasures: "… the soothing pint, the flickering hope of a good night's sleep." On our Prime Minister: "… he keeps his intelligence cunningly concealed." On the humourless: "… fuck them if they can't take a joke."

And so it goes. At the counter, a faithful employee has been on her feet for hours working the *order-here* line. She has a lovely smile and is careful to ask every customer, "Do youse want anything else?"

Goat Yoga

We were back at the Ikea cafeteria again this week for the chatter and the cheap curmudgeon's breakfast. They open at 9:30a.m., convenient for retired guys, and the parking lot is mostly empty, but you should make a mental note where you park, it may be filled when you come out. The cafeteria space is bright and optimistic with huge hanging lampshades, each the size of a Kyrgyzstan yurt. We fill our tray with the traditional breakfast and take a seat by the window. The vista from mountaintop shrine to consumerism is impressive, looking out across the parking lot at the retail giants in the distance, where Costco seems to be the mothership. There is new construction and imminent openings everywhere, but we don't pay any attention to the landscape. We focus on the scrambled eggs, bacon, and banter, and review recent news items.

Of course we touched on the June election when Ontarians gave Doug Ford a clear majority, where Kathleen declared prematurely she couldn't Wynne, where Horwath did well downtown and the Greenies won a seat in Guelph. And next door in Quebec at the G-7, Trump came late and left early, and (to the delight of his sycophants) threw a temper tantrum as he was leaving for Singapore. Apparently it was Michael Corleone who suggested it was good counsel to keep your friends close and your enemies closer, but in Quebec, Donald (a special-needs President) could only remember the latter half of this advice. And in Singapore, it remains to be seen if Kim outfoxed him … or maybe it was Xi Jinping (standing just offstage) who outfoxed them both. In any case, Trump feels a special bond with Kim, a kindred spirit with whom he shares a penchant for autocracy and bad haircuts.

Of course, Trump throwing a temper tantrum is neither surprising nor illegal, and it wouldn't matter if it was illegal because, as we now know, Trump has every right to pardon himself for high crimes and misdemeanors. (Albert pointed out that years ago, during his Catholic School education, this self-pardoning concept would have saved the priests a lot of time). And if the expansion of the power of the Executive Branch goes the way he plans, Mr. Trump will soon be able to heal himself––the blind will see, the lame will walk, lepers will be cleansed, and the good news will spread (on FOX) among the poor. For all intents and purposes, Trump has declared himself infallible, an attribute reserved, until recently, only for the Pope in Rome and Oprah Winfrey.

We nudged the conversation forward––the weather, changes in blood pressure and cholesterol medication, and an article from the *Herald* indicating men in Atlantic Canada are among the unhealthiest in captivity. Apparently, only about one man in sixteen is in the very healthy category. (We saw that guy this morning on the way into Ikea. He was walking up the stairs beside us. We were on the escalator.)

And it turns out we smoke too much, drink too much, and don't get enough exercise. We had no idea. It seemed like a lot of negativity––what about our self-esteem? The good news from the report is that about half of us sleep too little and half of us sleep too much, so that on average we are doing just fine. The study also pointed out that most of us are unhealthy eaters.

Albert paused, looked down at his bacon, munched it, and suggested remedial action. We could all improve our health and well-being, he said, if we started attending goat yoga. He pointed to the write-up that revealed goat yoga will soon be available at Sweetwood Farm in Lunenburg County where the owner is planning her first goat yoga event of the summer season. *Think about having four or five baby goats crawling all over you. That's pretty fantastic,* she said.

During a pause in the conversation, we looked around the cafeteria. Everyone seemed in good spirits, with one noticeable exception. At the table next to us, a woman who looked like Angela Merkel was standing, glaring down at her eggs, looking at them the way Merkel looks at Trump. The nature of her problem wasn't obvious. Was it some recent annoyance, or just her perpetual irritation at the burdens of existence? In any case, something made Angela very cranky (and her husband better not leave any teabags in the sink). Albert, with the milk of human kindness dripping from his chin, said we shouldn't be too quick to judge poor Angela. Who knows what mortifications caused her such distress—perhaps an ingrown toenail, or rectal polyps.

We changed the subject to electoral boundaries and processes, and Albert went off on a tangent reminding us that when his dear old mother (God rest her soul) was born, it was four years before Canadian women were allowed to vote and ten years before Nellie McClung convinced the Supreme Court that women really were persons.

This was Albert's way of introducing a news item from a couple months back, about an American animal rights organization seeking to change the legal status of chimpanzees to that of persons. The effort was supported by at least two philosophers at Dalhousie University who submitted an amicus brief to the appellate division of the New York Supreme Court, which had agreed to hear arguments brought on behalf of two plaintiffs — both of them chimpanzees.

We were willing to set aside the fact that doctors can't agree on whether or not milk is good for us, and talk about cows, free markets, supply-managed dairy, Maxime Bernier, and the independence of elected officials. And Bernier's fate (at the hands of Andrew Scheer) reminded us of recent media coverage cautioning concern for the erosion of democratic processes; the concentration of control in party leadership; the intrusions on independent thought and mindless endorsements for party leadership; and, most importantly, the impact on the very concept of representative democracy, where elected officials are supposed to represent the interests of their constituents, not their supreme leader. We agreed that this sobering and somewhat ominous topic will be included on future agendas.

Albert noted that the breakfast was good but that he missed the dark-roast coffee at Tim's, and he would be going through the drive-thru on his way home. Albert explained that he has a special relationship with the woman at the speaker.

She always tells me her name, and even when I am clearly done giving my order, she always asks if there is anything else I want. Then she tells me what kind of a day to have––very thoughtful.

Then Albert abruptly announced that, to ensure domestic tranquility and secure the blessings of liberty, he had to go home right away. He remembered that his wife needed the car for a specialist's appointment. Albert was lying when he claimed that he has recently started calling his wife MRI because, "just like that fancy machine at the hospital, she can see right through me and tell me what's wrong."

For retirees, the promise of a cheap breakfast is one of those temptations that can only be removed by giving in to it, which we think is the best way to get rid of most of them. We've been to the mountaintop; we'll be back again next week.

ASSORTED RUMINATIONS

Turning 70: The Side Effects

An increasing number of us are members of an elite group of chronological specialists who are lucky enough (think of the alternative) to turn seventy during this calendar year.

If you are among us, there's a good chance that you were born in 1949 (advanced mathematics), which is the year that Ireland became a republic, the Soviets tested an atomic bomb, Joseph Stalin attacked Russian Jews, the first credit card was issued, and Wile E. Coyote became a celebrity.

And in Washington, during 1949, the White House was completely gutted and then restored. God knows, it's time again.

When folks talk about our maturing demographic, seventy seems to be accepted as a marker of sorts, a milestone, or a millstone, signifying senescence.

Apparently seventy is our shelf life. The Bible says so (Psalm 90:10)—*threescore years and ten* is our allotted span. It is the scriptural statute of limitations. After that, we are released from active duty, put out to pasture, our regular time having expired. Everything after seventy is stoppage time, as in the World Cup of Soccer, you never know for sure when the game will be over, when you'll be flying home. In a few years, you may be sitting around the departure lounge hoping your flight will be delayed.

Reaching seventy required no great effort on my part. I did it in the usual way, without noticing, without any awareness of how it happened, just the ongoing accumulation of days and incredible good fortune, the care and feeding from my wife, my flourishing family, and no hang-gliding. There was a negligible contribution from me, and although I feel fortunate, *blessed among men*, I have to say the seventy marker feels different from the others. It's harder to blow out the candles.

Not only can this birthday be disconcerting, it can also be a little disappointing.

The day my friend Albert turned seventy, he tried to hint to his wife what he wanted for his birthday supper by wearing a lobster bib around the house all day long. Sadly, she never noticed the bib, and Albert had to settle for pork chops and mashed potatoes. And after dessert (bread pudding), when she presented him with a cordless drill, he never mentioned that he had his heart set on a new Toyota Tacoma, graciously hiding his disappointment until later in the evening when he and I were sharing a wee drop of Bushmills Black.

Albert and I were musing that lately the talk about aging has grown tedious, and current circumstances may warrant some legislative changes. We know the world belongs to the young people imagining themselves to have new ideas, so why not contemplate a few new rules for contrarians?

Sure, we are all equal under the law, but a few social and legal exemptions may be warranted for those over seventy. These revisions could be known as the 3-C laws (Curmudgeons, Contrarians, Coughers). We came up with a half-dozen examples.

Seniors would be authorized to arrive at (or leave) social events at any time for no reason, completely exempt from criticism. And at home, dinner guests and evening visitors—especially relatives—would be prohibited from staying overnight (grandchildren are the only exception) unless they have travelled over one thousand kilometers. Local guests would be required to leave by 9:30p.m.

Anyone over seventy will be permitted to dislike a fixed number of things and people without any justifiable reason, and without having to defend or explain their aversion. (To illustrate, we began a list that includes, among many others, the giggling people delivering the evening news, the Kardashians, registered aroma therapists, Oprah Winfrey, smiling politicians, world-savers, ostentatious moralists, and the guy on the Trivago ad. I could strangle that moron.)

A chronologically sensitive world also requires a few verbal embargoes. No one would be permitted to ask a senior, "Is it hot enough for ya?" or use the phrase "It is what it is." And restaurant servers who ask, "Any plans for the rest of the evening?" would, following conviction, serve weekends in custody.

Among publications directed at seniors, freedom of the press would be maintained, but two-word phrases where the adjective contradicts the noun would be excluded from usage and banned from publication. Examples of such oxymoronic pairs include: reality television, rap music, vegetable burger, progressive conservative, social science, charm offensive, objective journalism. There are many more.

And since the elderly sometimes tend to slur their words, they require more legal latitude on matters related to offending people in a public setting.

If during a period of inclement weather, an innocent comment to a woman on the airplane such as "Particularly harsh weather" comes out sounding like "*Tickle your arse with a feather?*," first-time offenders past seventy should be exempted from inclusion on the no-fly list.

And to avoid surges in high blood pressure while driving, certain roadside prohibitions are necessary. For example, the posting of stupid church signs (e.g. *God answers knee mail*) would be added to the Criminal Code. These people need jail time.

And in the domestic sphere, Albert and I believe some regulatory changes are required, especially protocols related to the fixed positioning of objects in the kitchen cupboards.

Peanut butter located in the corner cupboard for the past twenty-five years has to stay there — one can't just arbitrarily move peanut butter willy-nilly to the shelf by the fridge. And if, since Confederation, the sugar has been on the bottom shelf, two doors from the sink, what possible rationale would require it to be moved to the middle shelf?

I can't be squandering my time looking for the sugar. If the Bible is to be believed, I don't have much left.

Satisfaction Levels

Amid conflicting evidence, a serious study was recently concluded in Great Britain that reaffirmed a slice of popular wisdom. It turns out that your grandmother was right—apparently, *money can't buy happiness.*

At least this is true in the U.K., where the Office for National Statistics (ONS) compared happiness and household wealth and concluded that people are currently less happy (more anxious) despite significant increases in their disposable income.

With surprising precision, the ONS data has revealed that since 2012, the average person (in the U.K.) has become 36% wealthier, but only 3% happier—clearly a balance-of-trade deficit. Household wealth has continued to rise while happiness levels have flat-lined.

Some of us EONS (Elderly Ordinary Nova Scotians) are suspicious of these

ONS (Office of National Statistics) conclusions, and have reason to suspect that a moderate bit of affluence might cheer us up more than the researchers imagine.

And, as a result of our healthy skepticism, we think the money/happiness research should be replicated here in Nova Scotia. If Statistics Canada is interested, I am willing to round up a few volunteers (contemporaries) who are eager to participate in a controlled experiment—all in the name of scholarship and the inexorable advancement of science.

It would be a simple agreement. In a spirit of reciprocity, the government would provide us (the senior volunteers) with the resources required for a life of lavish extravagance and, in return, we would describe our happiness levels at regular intervals on a seven-point happiness scale: Despondent, Complacent, Content, Cheerful, Blissful, Ecstatic, Gaga.

To ensure validity, it would be a longitudinal study conducted over a ten-year period. Participants would endure the challenges of a life of shameless self-indulgence and indicate how they felt about it by submitting a report every month until the ten years expired, or the reporter expired, whichever came first.

There would be no penalty to any senior who failed to complete the ten-year term as a result of his or her passing, although the happiness quotient would be expected to decline and the reporting frequency reduced. No exit interview would be required.

Years ago, my mother (deceased) conveyed an unambiguous (some would say odd) point of view on the whole money/happiness correlation. Although I'm pretty sure she never read a social-science research summary, or imagined that happiness could be quantified, she would have mostly concurred with the recent findings of the ONS.

And while she certainly approved of ambition and achievement, and felt strongly that everyone deserved an equal opportunity to engage in the pursuit of happiness, she did not equate pursuit with acquisition. She never used the term *income inequality*, but she had an intuitive sense of the indignities that may result from it. She articulated her position with eloquence: *Everyone deserved to have a roof over their heads, food on the table, and a pot to piss in.*

When the piss-pot threshold was reached, there was some obligation to share. I'm not sure Mom's attitude represented an entire generation's, but I do know that she was a very smart woman with a strong, moral heritage and a peculiar attitude toward the well-off.

Her generation lived through the Great Depression and the aftermath of a world war. They knew what a day's work looked like. They understood scarcity during a period deprived of social safety nets, when the middle class was both inclusive and expansive. Parsimony and frugality were elements of character. *Minimalism*—while ever-present—was not a lifestyle choice.

Affluence made my mother suspicious. Vigilance was required because unfettered luxury could impair even the most principled person. Rich people lacked the sanctifying experiences of poverty. Impurities needed to be burned away in the furnace of adversity. We should pity those unfortunate souls who had never felt the sacred embrace of deprivation. Adversity allowed for the consolations of religion and faith.

Most especially, ostentatious prosperity had to be guarded against. Mom had no time for the muckety-mucks, or anyone on their high horse, or people with *more money than you could shake a stick at*. Instead, she felt an affinity with those whose lives were unsullied by the temptations of wealth and uncontaminated by the trappings of ostentation.

Mother noted a distinction between those who made money (bankers) and those who earned money (farmers). In her universe, material success could be tolerated only as a result of hard work and virtue. Neither being *born to privilege* or having it *thrust upon you* was acceptable. If you wanted a pot to piss in, you had to find your own. In this way, you could avoid the sin of covetousness (It's the Tenth Commandment).

Ma took the ONS research conclusions one step further—not only did money not buy happiness, it could, under some circumstances, provide an impediment. She sought to remove all impediments. *Lilies grow from poor soil,* she said, *and money has no manners.*

And following reminders that *not by bread alone doth man live*, she'd claim that *prosperity is bad for your digestion—because, you know, all that rich food.*

I'm not sure if mother's judgment on these matters was contaminated by our Irish heritage (resentment, like guilt, was important to the Irish—Irish begrudgery), or the concealed envy that's part of human nature, or her own (materially) humble childhood.

Sometimes it seemed that Mom didn't really trust happiness anyway. It was so unreliable (*misery, now there's something you can count on*). Poverty always had companions; affluence can be so isolating and severe.

For her, it was more about the striving, the satisfaction or contentment for having done something, or having given something. And more than money, laughing about ourselves and making fun of others seemed essential to human happiness. Whatever Mom's scarcities, generosity was not one of them. She had a remarkable ability to make everyone around her feel better––kindness, for her, was more a pleasure than a duty.

Back to our proposed research study: I'd still be willing to give it a shot.

I think my lovely old mom (she was a handsome woman in her day) wouldn't really mind if I participated in the money/happiness experiment. Above all else, she wanted her children to be happy. And happiness, she felt, was something we all could achieve if we just made up our minds. Mother might be right.

My next-door neighbour is from Newfoundland. Every time I see him (often), I ask him, "How ya doin' today, Robert?"

He always has the same enthusiastic answer. "Best day a me life, bye. Best day a me life."

See what I mean?

Elusive Truth

Many of my generation are non-Facebookers, surviving members of the last cohort that will (following expiration) leave behind only a faint electronic footprint. Every subsequent generation is condemned to a comprehensive virtual record that could last for *eternity,* which (as Woody Allen says) *is a very long time, especially towards the end.*

For many of us, our meagre record in the cyberworld is something we are thankful for. The things we did, said, and thought when we were young (and knew everything) warrant complete eradication, and provoke a bit of a shudder when we imagine that our feeble adolescent musings could be reviewed by children and grandchildren. Among seniors, contentment involves good health and bad memory.

On the other hand, limited access to social media (tweeting, twittering, blogging, clogging, flogging), coupled with diminished capacity, may leave us disadvantaged when we feel compelled to comment on the health of our province, surrounded as it is by an encroaching ocean and mounting debt.

And when we non-pundits imagine even minor commentary on the fragile state of our democracy, we often feel (due to technical deficits) ill-equipped, as hindered as a government backbencher, as hampered as October apples.

In any case, there are a few folks like me (and Will Rogers) who only know what we read in the papers (Rogers claimed it was an alibi for his ignorance), so there's a good chance that my commentary is misguided.

No matter.

These days, we hear a lot about ordinary people losing faith in democratic institutions. Astute political observers warn us about legislative assemblies where the only obligation of elected members is to repeat a scripted, uncritical echo of party leadership, and where obsequious backbenchers surrender the prospect of making up their own minds.

Here in Nova Scotia, our auditor general laments ambiguous financial controls, the privacy commissioner is denied access to information held by the health minister, government members attempt to control the agenda at the public accounts committee, and elected school boards are eliminated while government consolidates control of public education and chips away at union membership.

We're not sure exactly where the money for Nova Scotia health authority Christmas parties came from, or what savings and efficiencies have accrued from consolidation, or what precisely is the cost-benefit analysis of the Yarmouth ferry, or what those P-3 schools really cost us, or when someone will articulate the merits of private hospital partnerships.

And we don't know why recruiters leave the NSHA, and we're not clear why we can't know why. It seems public scrutiny has become an irritation. Sometimes there are legitimate reasons, but the shelters of *commercial confidentiality, personnel issues, and privacy concerns* appear to be overworked.

As a starting point, the general rule might be that taxpayers are always allowed to ask about how their money is spent, and if this information is denied or delayed, then they can ask again, until a complete explanation is offered and accepted. It seems simple enough.

It's possible that ordinary Nova Scotians could penetrate the mysteries of debt servicing, payroll rebates, subsidized multinationals, and possibly even the arcane world of P-3 construction financing.

Governments like to talk about the value of candor and transparency. These are not new ideas. The honourable men and women who represent us in legislatures do not, for the most part, indulge in outright duplicity or malicious deceit. They are decent people commendably engaged in public service. But there is some evidence that they are susceptible to the temptations of selective recall, discretionary embellishment, and cloudy obfuscation.

Sometimes obfuscation pushes up against mendacity, and when fudging facts drifts toward fibbing, elected officials need to be careful––there is no need to amplify current levels of cynicism. Truth-telling is a good habit to get into (glance southward to see what happens when voters are unencumbered by reality).

Legislators appear to believe that the truth is adequate in most circumstances but insufficient in others. They would like to tell the truth, but can't risk the consequences.

Remedial measures may be required. Before rising to speak in the House, members should have to swear a solemn oath, or at least cross their hearts and hope to die. This would also prevent their pants from catching on fire. Carelessness with the truth needs to be guarded against. Careless-truth politics is a running mate to a careless democracy.

It's a delicate business to tell the truth about lying. We've got half-truths, enduring truths, simple truths, provisional truths, profound truths, and lots of things that are *only true-up-to-a-point*.

Truth is shaped by time and place, and often allied to its source—we are reluctant to accept guidance and gospel from someone we don't like, and we embellish insights from those we do.

And lies are shape-shifters that come in a variety of colours. Lies can be red or blue depending on election results. White lies are forgivable and sometimes praiseworthy. Among the Irish, lies are available in white, green, and orange, and must be, by statute, entertaining (among Irish storytellers, truth is avoided as a matter of principle).

Some lies are harmless—when the person at the front of the meeting room tells you how much they'd like to have your input, it may be a bold-faced lie but it's nothing to get excited about. This is a standardized, garden-variety lie.

There are other subtleties. Political ambiguity is particularly nuanced. It must be seasonally adjusted; prevarication stridently rebuked in the spring is perfectly acceptable during a fall election. Campaigners should know that interest-bearing lies result in harm that is compounded and indexed to inflation.

There is no shortage of advice surrounding mendacity. Shakespeare warned us about tangled webs of deception. Thomas Hobbes suggested that *hell is truth seen too late*. Napoleon claimed *history is the set of lies agreed upon*. George Bernard Shaw told us *the liar's punishment isn't that he is not believed, but that he can't believe anyone else.*

And although I have manufactured a few realities and fabricated my share of anecdotes, I concede that my falsehood fluency is restricted because I have never served in government or studied political science at the university level.

I'm told that white lies (*the truth for the time being*) are told by honourable people simply exercising discretion. Any form of exercise is beneficial. These days, I get my exercise by walking upstairs or putting on my glasses. I tell a few lies, but mostly out of kindness or laziness. I try to avoid the malicious variety.

The ambiguities of deceit take a toll on delicate and sensitive seniors, but truth-telling often works out better than expected. It can even be career-enhancing. I'm considering a late-in-life profession change based on advice from my friend Willie Nelson who, at the age of eighty-five, says that anyone can write a good country song; *all you need are three cords and the truth.*

Even my saintly mother understood the contradictions and ambiguities of truth-telling. *You should always tell the truth,* she said, *or something close to it.* This is good advice.

Here's some more good advice. On a windy day, avoid the black rocks at Peggy's Cove, not only to avoid a watery death, but because your Donegal tweed cap keeps blowing off.

Awaiting My Epiphany

Challenging for the Democratic presidential nomination, former U.S. Vice President Joe Biden recently expressed optimism about the likelihood of bipartisan co-operation following the election in 2020.

He predicted that when the current president is defeated, *you will see an epiphany occur among many of my Republican friends.*

It seems unlikely.

In my experience (I could be an outlier), spontaneous flashes of inspiration are as scarce as hen's teeth. Regarding epiphanies, I'm skeptical.

But apparently, there are a few epiphanies going around these days, and lots of examples are celebrated from the past. Isaac Newton experienced such a phenomenon when an apple fell on his head, as did Ben Franklin while he was flying a kite. And what about Archimedes when he shouted "*Eureka!*" in his ancient Greek bathtub. (He emerged bathed in the afterglow of his awakening.)

And from classical literature, Scrooge experienced a powerful awakening related to Christmas, as did Hamlet when he started to realize that revenge wasn't the answer after all. And from the Bible, the original epiphany when the Magi, seeing a divine star in the sky, are led to the Christ child and his nature is suddenly revealed to them.

From Donegal, there's an agreeable story that involves an elderly Irishman describing how he sat bolt upright in bed one night, startled by an unexpected awareness. *It suddenly occurred to me that I have never in my life had an epiphany. It came to me right out of the blue.*

Like the Irishman, I'm not sure if I'd recognize an epiphany if I fell on it. It takes me a long time to have sudden realizations. Some folks suggest that epiphanies are more likely to occur in the exuberance of youth. Scrounging around in my distant past, I recently went looking for awakenings and couldn't find any.

Insights from earlier times (such as they were) seem incremental and almost imperceptible. Few turning points are remembered. I don't recall any social upheavals. No revelations on my Road to Damascus. At no point did scales fall from my eyes.

But I later learned that during the period of my adolescence, there was a whole lot of stuff going on. I can only conclude that at the time I wasn't paying attention.

I grew up in the 1950s and 1960s, and lately I've been reading about some of the social, technological, and political developments that characterized the Canadian experience way back then. Canadians were busy during the middle of the last century.

At the time, I knew nothing about Canadians' post-war appetite for consumer products, or the dynamism that transformed our economy, or the increasingly influential media and communication industries, or the burgeoning affluence of the middle class. I was mostly unaware of the emerging cultural influences of McDonald's restaurants, Holiday Inns, rock 'n' roll, Motown music, and the hula hoop.

I was oblivious to the social influences resulting from exuberant consumerism, the anxieties of the Cold War, the genesis of the Space Age, the emergence of the Beat Generation, the sexual revolution, the stirrings of feminism, and the war in Vietnam.

And I paid no attention to the emerging global perils: insidious communism, the decay of social structures, the dangers of a Sino-Soviet Alliance, the development of the hydrogen bomb, the emerging military-industrial state in America, and the CIA activity in Iran and Guatemala.

Not once did I march in the streets to protest the avarice of capitalism, the proliferation of nuclear weapons, or the segregation of the races. I didn't care about the war in Vietnam, and never once reflected on the alienation and estrangement of modern life. For the first twenty years of my life, I didn't know I was part of a post-war birth phenomenon—a baby boomer.

Glancing backward through my sheltered adolescence, no barriers were broken down, no taboos were trampled on, and as far as I can remember, no shockwaves ripped through the seams of my daily life. I don't recall (as memoirists of the 1950s and 1960s suggest) being thrust into a new world.

Likewise, the adults around me gave the impression that nothing was revealed to them suddenly and effortlessly. They seemed to think understanding developed slowly and deliberately, and would be refined, improved, or abandoned over time as new experiences informed. Excellence was the result of extended periods of study and reflection rather than out-of-the-blue flashes of inspiration. Progress involved iterations and rehearsals—*on stepping stones, we rise to grander things.*

"Put your head down and go to work," my father used to say. He seemed to trust perspiration above inspiration.

Maybe this is all part of some misremembered past. I can't be sure. In any case, I'm still waiting for my flash of insight, my moment of clarity.

Some people a lot smarter than I am suggest that it's not about momentary occurrences at all, that life, from birth to death, is a continuing epiphany, an ongoing awakening. Maybe so.

For me, so far, useful insights (if they show up at all) have arrived incrementally. They leave the same way.

I'm waiting patiently. I want an epiphany of my own. I want a flash of inspiration. I want to be like the dedicated environmentalist who claimed that his passion was the result of an energy-efficient light bulb going off in his head.

Now, to encourage such an unearned and unexpected moment of clarity, I'm heading now for my big La-Z-Boy chair. For some time, my circadian rhythms have included an afternoon nap. Maybe a sleep will provoke an awakening. It's worth a shot.

I may have to wait until the cows come home.

Humility: Still a Virtue

On Saturday afternoon, while I was waiting for my friend Albert to join me in my garage for a beer, I was thinking about my long-departed father who was born in 1919 while the ink was drying on the Treaty of Versailles. My father felt strongly about doing things right. He didn't talk much.

In Nova Scotia, there's a good chance that our burgeoning population of retirees experienced fathers (like mine) who were reticent, taciturn, and withholding. Theirs was a generation not given to ostentation and effusion. These men didn't spill over with words and emotions. Quiet reserve was considered a virtue. And among these fathers, born between the world wars, unobtrusive humility was well-regarded.

There were rules: You should convey a quiet confidence in your abilities, but avoid pretention and affectation. Don't call attention to yourself. Stand up for yourself, but stay off your high horse––self-promotion and self-pity are not acceptable. For the most part, you should put your head down and go to work. Putting on the dog was also a felony.

(These are the quiet fathers described with poignancy in Ernest Buckler's short story "Penny in the Dust," and in Robert Hayden's poem "Those Winter Sundays.")

Of course, not all of their quiet reserve was beneficial; approaches to parenting may have improved. Silent reticence can deepen the divide between fathers and children. Laconic, monosyllabic men did not always facilitate family harmony. And the tendency to amplify virtues of an idealized past needs to be guarded against.

Nonetheless, the passage of time is not the same as progress, and there remains some attraction for an era when humility was a sign of strength, not weakness. The reticence of past generations was not necessarily callousness, neither was their modesty submissive nor their humility obsequious.

To that generation, much of today's culture would be alien. We now seem keen on aggressive self-promotion, decisive boldness, and a win-at-all-cost mentality. The demeanor of successful people is rarely characterized by modesty. Crassness and coarseness has infiltrated public life. We esteem those who walk with a swagger in their step, grandstanding legends in their own mind. There is little evidence that *the meek are blessed*, or that *they will inherit the earth*.

And nowadays, rather than achieve greatness, some prefer to thrust it upon themselves. Public figures (in a range of categories) assign to themselves an extravagant self-assessment, amplified by ego and undiminished by reality.

We sanction a popular culture where real housewives are awarded their own TV programs to flaunt hedonistic lifestyles and conduct their juvenile squabbles for the public to enjoy.

We keep up with talentless pseudo-celebrities who have accomplished nothing (except their own celebrity), happy to showcase the excesses and indulgences of their lives.

Professional athletes dance and strut and look to the crowd for adulation when they do their job (catch a football, sack a quarterback), and wealthy team owners feel entitled to taxpayers' dollars to subsidize their investments.

And it seems we have nurtured a political culture that produces leadership unrestricted by embarrassment or shame. Our retired Governor General imagines her ongoing contributions to the nation warrant a six-figure expense account to supplement her six-figure salary.

Our Prime Minister (the Leader Dude) supposes his unimprovable face should grace the front cover of *GQ* magazine. A former federal government minister imagines his physical plant so dazzling that photographs should be texted to young women. CEOs consider their inscrutable business acumen so valuable it should be compensated with incomes a thousand times that of dairy farmers. Representative governments act as if they believe the people they represent aren't smart enough to be told what's really going on.

And, of course, the American President––the antithesis of humility––is the leader of the arrogance ascendency, as well as the free world. He believes any mention of human weakness or vulnerability is *loser talk*. The President thinks humility is a four-letter word. He's not much of a speller, but we do know that if he wanted to be humble, he would be the most humble person in the world. He would brag and crow about his humility, and he wouldn't detect the irony.

Hubris is not an asset, and humility is not a character flaw. In fact, humility is necessary not only for productive social interaction but also for learning. It allows us to think well enough of others to believe they have something valuable to teach us.

My father insisted that if we listen hard enough, we have something to learn from everyone we meet. It is, as Winston Churchill said, the greatest lesson in life to know that *even fools are right sometimes*. My father would have agreed with Churchill by quietly nodding his head.

Common sense is available to everyone, but it comes gradually. And the wisdom that allegedly comes with age, if it comes at all, probably includes the realization that we have no choice but to be humble. It can't be otherwise. The world is too complex. It has too many ambiguities and contradictions, too many unanswered questions––only fools and fanatics are sure of everything.

And as our insufficiencies become more obvious and our limitations more acute, we begin to understand that we're all pretty much in the same boat. If nothing else, the accumulation of years is the great levelling experience.

If the trajectory of a life includes aspiration, attainment, and quiet reflection, then part of late-onset contemplation might include a newfound humility which, in one sense, softens our decline.

CPSIA information can be obtained
at www.ICGtesting.com
Printed in the USA
BVHW071504251120
594058BV00001B/75

9 781525 573514